T0324349

Abolishing Freedom

SERIES EDITORS · *Marco Abel and Roland Végső*

PROV
OCAT
IONS

Something in the world forces us to think.
—Gilles Deleuze

The world provokes thought. Thinking is nothing but the human response to this provocation. Thus the very nature of thought is to be the product of a provocation. This is why a genuine act of provocation cannot be the empty rhetorical gesture of the contrarian. It must be an experimental response to the historical necessity to act. Unlike the contrarian, we refuse to reduce provocation to a passive noun or a state of being. We believe that real moments of provocation are constituted by a series of actions that are best defined by verbs or even infinitives—verbs in a modality of potentiality, of the promise of action. To provoke is to intervene in the present by invoking an as yet undecided future radically different from what is declared to be possible in the present and, in so doing, to arouse the desire for bringing about change. By publishing short books from multiple disciplinary perspectives that are closer to the genres of the manifesto, the polemical essay, the intervention, and the pamphlet than to traditional scholarly monographs, "Provocations" hopes to serve as a forum for the kind of theoretical experimentation that we consider to be the very essence of thought.

www.provocationsbooks.com

Abolishing Freedom

A Plea for a Contemporary Use of Fatalism

FRANK RUDA

UNIVERSITY OF NEBRASKA PRESS · LINCOLN AND LONDON

The series editors would like to thank
Jaime Brunton, Daniel Clausen, Daniel
Froid, Robert Lipscomb, and Edwardo Rios
for their work on the manuscript. This
initial volume of the series is dedicated
to the memory of Ernesto Laclau.

Library of Congress
Cataloging-in-Publication Data

Names: Ruda, Frank, author.
Title: Abolishing freedom: a plea for a
contemporary use of fatalism / Frank Ruda.
Description: Lincoln: University of
Nebraska Press, 2016. | Series:
Provocations | Includes
bibliographical references.
Identifiers: LCCN 2015049866
ISBN 9780803284371 (pbk.: alk. paper)
ISBN 9780803288782 (ePub)
ISBN 9780803288799 (mobi)
ISBN 9780803288805 (pdf)
Subjects: LCSH: Fate and fatalism. | Liberty.
Classification: LCC BJ1468.5 .R83 2016
DDC 149/.8—dc23 LC record available
at http://lccn.loc.gov/2015049866

Set in Sorts Mill Goudy by Rachel Gould.
Designed by N. Putens.

To Eva, for teaching me that the worst always already happened

In our times we can neither endure our faults nor the means of correcting them.

—Titus Livy

CONTENTS

ACKNOWLEDGMENTS

Even fatalists can be grateful. And if they believe that the worst has always already happened, they are grateful to those who in their respective ways made (thinking) the worst possible. They form something like a gang of the worst: a club that consists only of members who, following Groucho Marx's famous saying, would never become members of a club that would take them as members. For me this impossible club includes Eva Heubach, Marco Abel, Alain Badiou, Georg W. Bertram, Lorenzo Chiesa, Rebecca Comay, Joan Copjec, Mladen Dolar, Lorenz Engell, Simon Hajdini, Agon Hamza, Fredric Jameson, Christoph Menke, Mark Potocnik, Ozren Pupovac, Rado Riha, Aaron Schuster, Jelica Šumič, Roland Végső, Christiane Voss, Alenka Zupančič, Slavoj Žižek, and Hugo Heubach.

Today freedom has become a signifier of oppression. In this historical situation fatalism is the only possible stance that allows us to think freedom without being indifferent. We must affirm the position of a *comic fatalism*, whose slogans are:

Start by expecting the worst!
Act as if you did not exist!
Act as if you were not free!
Act in such a way that you accept the struggle you cannot flee from!
Act in such a way that you never forget to imagine the end of all things!
Act as if the apocalypse has already happened!
Act as if everything were always already lost!
Act as if you were dead!
Act as if you were an inexistent woman!

Abolishing Freedom

Introduction

Fatalism in Times of Universalized Assthetization

> *Heaven which wants! We never know what Heaven wants or*
> *doesn't want, and perhaps Heaven doesn't even know itself.*
> —Denis Diderot, *Jacques the Fatalist and His Master*

Nothing, less than nothing, without any further determination.
This book will argue that any rationalist should start from this
assumption in order to conceptualize freedom. *Fatalism, the pure
fatalism* it will defend, aims at abolishing freedom in all prevail-
ing senses of the term. The motivation for beginning this book
in such an apparently unappealing way is linked to a diagnosis
shared by many contemporary thinkers, namely that "freedom"
became (or is) a signifier of disorientation. As a result the signifier *freedom* can function as a signifier of disorientation, that is,
in an utterly repressive way. But how could one not be in favor
of freedom? In an age when freedom functions as a signifier
that enables the dismantling of all forms of social protection,
it is important to understand how freedom effectively works.
The fact that today people often get only temporary job con-
tracts, for instance, is presented to us as an opportunity to freely
explore different job opportunities. Similarly the implementa-
tion of universal health care in the United States was attacked
by stating that only in the absence of such a system is one free

to choose the health care one actually wants. We may recall here what Karl Marx had already claimed in the first volume of his *Critique of Political Economy*. Within the exchange relation between the worker and the capitalist, there "is in fact a very Eden of the innate rights of man. There alone rule Freedom, Equality, Property and Bentham."[1] The name of the utilitarian philosopher indicates what is constitutive of the series of these concepts.[2] Later Marx and Engels stated even more explicitly in the *Communist Manifesto*, "By freedom is meant—under the present bourgeois conditions of production—free trade, free selling and buying."[3] The freedom of most people consists in their freedom to sell their labor power (which appears to them as simply a necessity, given that not doing so would endanger their ability to subsist). The freedom of the capitalist, on the other hand, consists of freely buying another person's labor power. There is, then, a fundamental equality among the two groups of free agents involved in this exchange—yet one profits from this arrangement, whereas the other has no choice but to engage in it.

But what are the conceptual foundations of this arrangement? I will argue that one fundamental conceptual maneuver that is necessarily involved in turning freedom into a signifier of disorientation is the tendency to understand freedom in terms of a capacity that one has. However, by defining freedom as a personal capacity, we turn freedom into something that a person has and owns—something that is someone's property and can be invested in multiple ways. But there is another consequence of this definition of freedom. As soon as we understand freedom as a capacity (that may be realized whenever and in whichever way), we assume that freedom is not only a capacity but also a possibility. But by understanding freedom as a possibility, we conceive of it as already being real and actual in the form of this possibility (that then can be actualized). Reduced to being a capacity, freedom already has its reality (maybe even its full reality) in its possibility. With this conceptual move, freedom as possibility is identified with freedom as actuality. This, however, is a conflation because it leads to the idea that freedom is already real without actually being realized. Against this conflation, which is, as I will argue, fundamentally Aristotelian in nature, this book will attempt to exorcise the last remaining bits of Aristotelianism from contemporary thought. To put it simply, this book seeks to be fundamentally anti-Aristotelian.

In philosophy this feature of Aristotelianism has recently become a common thread of even the most opposed camps: on one side, people start from the assumption that human beings are always already inscribed into a space of reasons (and thereby cannot but realize reason, since any step they take occurs within this space); on the other, people assume that being as such is dynamic and allows for certain realizations. Both sides identify being with time as the ultimate version of possibility and thereby are both radically Aristotelian in nature.

One name for the conceptual conflation at work in nearly any kind of Aristotelianism, be it of a naturalistic or of a transcendental kind, is "freedom of choice."[4] A result of understanding freedom as freedom of choice that is already actualized in *having* a choice (and thus before actually making it) is "indifference."[5] This is at least an often repeated claim that one finds in the history of philosophy, from Descartes through Kant to Hegel. And this "spread of indifference in European civilization"— that Marx and Badiou describe as a gigantic production and administration of indifference—might have its origins in an essential misunderstanding of the notion of freedom.[6] The French philosopher Gilles Châtelet depicted the result of this misunderstanding in his last book by means of a brutal yet beautiful slogan, which refers back to the old Platonic debate between Socrates and Glaucon.[7] If we identify freedom with a capacity, Châtelet writes, we start "to live and think like pigs."[8] Marx himself already demonstrated that within bourgeois societies man is ultimately reduced to being an animal. But things are more complicated. We are not simply reduced to a given form of animality—for example, in Kantian terms, to our pathological inclinations and needs that are ultimately always the exact opposite of freedom—but rather to an animality that is produced by and within the very same act by means of which we are reduced. If, however, we take seriously the diagnosis of the present state of indifference, the animality that is produced and to which we are reduced can paradigmatically be represented more adequately by having recourse not to the pig but to the donkey: to the ass. In an infamous logical anecdote, often (falsely) attributed to Johannes Buridan, the so-called Buridan's ass finds itself in the following situation: it is hungry, and in front of it equidistantly are two equally tempting bales of hay. Being unable to decide which of the two to approach, the ass ultimately starves to death. Usually this anecdote is taken to exemplify a logical problem inherent in an understanding of freedom as freedom of choice.[9] If indifference results from understanding freedom as a capacity that one has, namely to choose freely, then freedom itself is mortified and dies, so to speak, for even if concrete choices are taken, they are taken in such a way that freedom ultimately disappears. In this precise sense, then, the present situation can be said to be a *time of universalized assthetization.*

Yet the story of Buridan's ass also implies that a true decision is always based on a paradox. By starving to death and not making a decision, the ass makes the decision not to opt for either of the two options at hand. Two things follow from this refusal. First, as already stated, the freedom of choice is really identical to a nonchoice that deadens freedom. Second, there is also a choice on a level that is more fundamental than the two options presented as constituting the choice. It is precisely the latter choice—choosing to be unable to choose—that the present book sees as a way out of the impasse of identifying freedom with the freedom of choice. The name I assign to this solution is *fatalism*. To be explicit: I do not defend any Hölderlinian paradigm of thought (politics, etc.) that would assume that "where danger is, grows the saving power also." I am rather straightforwardly arguing for fighting fire with fire.

To make this move more intelligible, let us briefly turn to *Florville and Courval, or Fatality*, a rarely discussed novella by the Marquis de Sade.[10] It tells the story of an aristocrat, Courval, who decides to remarry years after his wife, whom he assumes dead, left him. The two children they had, a boy and a girl, also "disappeared." They lost the girl early, and the boy left Courval at age fifteen for a life of his own. Courval's story will turn out to be a very peculiar comedy of remarriage.[11] Everything begins when he seems to have found the perfect woman: Florville, thirty-six years old, whose only blemishes seem to be that her ancestry is unknown, although she is recognized as the cousin of a reputable man called Saint-Prât, and that at the age of sixteen she had a child who later died. Apart from these two flaws, she appears to be an angel walking the earth. After witnessing her nobility and grace, Courval decides to marry her. Florville agrees but wants to tell him her life story, which she begins with a confession. She is not Saint-Prât's cousin and does not know her ancestry. Abandoned as a baby, she was adopted by him but had to leave at the age of fifteen and was sent to his sister, who propagated promiscuity and coupled Florville with a young man. She became pregnant with a boy, but the young man abandoned her quickly and took their son with him. Florville went to a pious relative of Saint-Prât, with whom she spent the next few years. This relative delighted in worshiping God and loved to quote Pascal's famous argument: "If there is no God, what difference does believing in him make, where is the harm in doing so? But if there is a God, what danger do you not run by refusing to give him your faith?" At age thirty-four Florville met a young man who fell for her. She rejected him, but one night he tried to rape her. In self-defense she stabbed him, and he died from the attack. Florville left the pious relative, and while staying at a nearby hotel, she accidentally saw a woman stabbing someone. The murderer was arrested, and because of Florville's testimony, she was sentenced to death.

After listening to her story, Courval is still inclined to marry her, as he sees only tragic accidents that are not her fault.

One day, after the wedding, Courval's son, Senneval, comes to see him to report a family catastrophe. He explains that he himself had a son whom he placed in the care of a woman, but when he returned to pick him up, the child had been killed by a woman whom it tried to rape. Afterward Senneval learned that also his mother had been sentenced to death for committing a murder. In her last moments she told him that he had a sister whom she gave away as a baby to Saint-Prât. Florville, recognizing Senneval as the father of her son, exclaims, "Those are my crimes. . . . Either I see my lover in my brother or I see my husband in my father. . . . I see only the execrable monster who stabbed her own son and sentenced her mother to death." She grabs a pistol and commits suicide.

Florville's fantastic story is truly excessive. When all identities are revealed at the end, we learn that, without knowing it, she had killed her mother, had a child with her brother, was raped by her own child, whom she then killed, and finally married her own father. Everything moves from bad to worse, yet all of this is the result of nothing but the best of intentions. It is a catastrophic story apropos of which I am tempted to return to the Pascalian questions: If there is no God and instead only free choice, what difference does believing in God make? Where is the harm in doing so? First answer: If we believe in God even though he does not exist, and because of our free acts we end up killing and fucking our relatives, the harm linked to our belief lies in our not assuming full responsibility for our actions by attributing them to God's mysterious ways (or some deeper meaning of his plans). But if there is a God, what danger do we run by refusing to give him our faith? Second answer: If we do not believe in God only in our unfettered freedom, it is possible that by refusing to give him our faith we end up with a punishment (killing and fucking relatives) that we brought upon ourselves. A third answer might be: There is a God in whom we believe, but our belief is useless, as he cannot or will not help us. Perhaps he does not care, or perhaps he hates mankind. If there were a God Florville should believe in, would he not be such a sadistic one?

It is no surprise that this novella was written by the Marquis de Sade. Florville's God must be "a Supreme Being of Wickedness," the center of a "destructive theology," a sadist who makes this extended and intensified version of Oedipus possible.[12] Intensified because Florville not only kills her mother *and* her son but also sleeps with her father *and* her brother. She does the same thing as Oedipus but in an inverted form—and she does it twice. The intensification is linked to repetition with a difference (father *and* brother, etc.). We are confronted not only with Florville's acts but also with a father marrying his daughter, with a brother seducing and impregnating her sister, with a son raping his mother, and with a mother giving away her child. It seems as if the Oedipal structure expanded in all directions, and the very attempt to get rid of it inaugurated or reinforced it. The Oedipus one encounters in Florville's story is thereby already post-Oedipal.

We also encounter here a series of peculiar repetitions: Florville's son repeats the passion of his father (Senneval) and grandfather (Courval), who in turn repeats the passion of the other two. Or, the other way round, since we are dealing with a repetition that inverts the logical order of filiation and obfuscates who repeats whom: a *perverted repetition*. Florville's mother repeats Florville's crime (killing a woman), who already repeated and realized the *intended* killing of herself by the mother—an *inverted repetition* in which Florville repeats a deed never done (killing her child), thus realizing what was only intended before. She does what the mother had planned to do and thereby kills not only her child but also her mother. Florville, in turn, also repeats the act of having sex with a relative: with her brother, with her son, and with her father—a *compulsive repetition*. We encounter here "an interruption of the natural cycle of generation and destruction."[13] This cycle of repetitions suspends biological filiation and logical succession and even the logic of repetition itself: there is a repetition that strangely precedes what it repeats.

Because of this strange repetition, things turn from worse to worst and "point toward something like an unthinkable, indeed impossible excess," which grounds the intensifying series of wrongdoings that ends up being so excessively tragic that it is actually comic.[14] We could hardly imagine a worse outcome. And the worst of the worst seems to lie in the fact that we (like the characters) get to know only at the end that the worst did already happen—a slight change of perspective that changes everything. Prior to this discovery readers are likely to assume that all might end well. But would not everything change in advance if we were to change this assumption? Nobody anticipates that we can "only make a choice between various sorts of evil."[15] Hope (for happiness, etc.) seems to offer here a new horizon, only to crush the individuals even more thoroughly. It is by virtue of this very hope that we avoid assuming the (knowledge that the) worst (had already happened). Following this logic, Florville brings about her own fate precisely by her hopeful attempts to influence it. The true moral of the story, therefore, seems to lie in the idea that a really virtuous act should always start from the assumption that no matter what I do, I will ultimately end up being raped by my son, having sex with my brother and father, and killing my mother and son. Virtue seems to be possible only if we start from this assumption, that is, from assuming its impossibility.

This means that the only God one can believe in is a wicked God embodying "the dark excess of a ruthless divine sadism."[16] This insight forms the foundation of Sade's "truly transcendental fatalism."[17] His fatalism becomes explicit at the end of the novella, which takes up the famous saying of the chorus from Sophocles's *Oedipus at Colonus*: "Not to be born is, past all prizing, best. . . . The next best by far, that with all speed he should go thither, whence he hath come."[18] Kathy Acker is thus right to claim, "Sade wanted to show or to teach us who we are; he wanted for us to learn to want to not exist."[19] To learn to want to not exist is a lesson one can derive from assuming that the worst did already happen and there is no hope to ever transcend this world or, what we could also call in an ugly neologism, the *worldst*. Transcendental fatalism thus needs to be a fatalism of transcendence.

The present book adopts this idea and therefore defends fatalism not only as a means of countering indifference and the identification of freedom with a given capacity but also as the very precondition for articulating the proper concept of freedom. I therefore do not claim to develop here a concept of freedom, even though I will occasionally refer to some of its crucial components. I will only delineate its necessary prerequisites. I will argue that fatalism is an assumption that makes it possible to prepare for what one cannot prepare for—that is, for what Badiou calls an "event." My argument resembles to some extent what Jean-Pierre Dupuy calls "enlightened doom-saying."[20] Dupuy argues that what might seem impossible, namely a final (for example, ecological) catastrophe that would end the present order of things, is nonetheless absolutely certain based on our present knowledge. Assuming that this catastrophe is our destiny might then retroactively change the conditions of possibility of this very destiny. It may retroactively make it possible to change what appears to us as fate. My argument also bears a strong similarity to what Slavoj Žižek calls the "inversion of the apocalypse"—a maneuver that does not take the apocalypse as something that we will have to face in the future but as something that already took place.[21]

The ultimate philosophical figure for this retroactive inversion, the thinker who, strictly speaking, invented it, is Hegel. The present book is therefore written in a Hegelian spirit (Was there ever any other?) and, methodologically speaking, seeks to present a kind of Hegelian counterhistory of rationalism in philosophy. Yet the term *counterhistory* should not be understood in a Foucauldian sense, which would try to excavate the lives of those infamous men who have been touched by power but were immediately buried by it.[22] Rather the counterhistory presented here first and foremost takes up one trivial and completely obvious fact from the history of philosophical rationalism, a fact so obvious that almost everyone has ignored it. I am talking about the fact that the most (in)famous rationalists in Western philosophy (for example, Descartes, Kant, and Hegel) were not only defenders of reason and freedom but also defenders of predestination, divine providence, and fate.

The crucial but simple conceptual question this book raises is how we can bring together predestination, freedom, and reason. If we can show in a consistent manner that the great philosophers of rationalism and of freedom were at the same time fatalists, then we will also have the necessary conceptual means to intervene against the problematic conception of freedom that identifies it with a capacity. This will provide us with the means to abolish this conception of freedom. My aim is therefore to retrieve this philosophical fatalism in order to counter the conceptual conflation that results in indifference. My argument for fatalism as a precondition of freedom will unfold by mimicking—in a much abbreviated way—Hegel's own history of philosophy, a history that in its own terms is also a counterhistory. I will therefore reconstruct a certain number of paradigmatic positions within the history of rationalism—those of Descartes, Kant, and Hegel—and end with a chapter on Freud. But because Hegel himself claimed that it is philosophy's task to articulate in the medium of the concept what Luther articulated in the medium of feeling, I begin with a chapter on Luther.

The history presented here is also conceived as counterhistory because it is a *history of worsening*. This does not simply mean that things gets continually worse but that this book presents successive positions on how we can understand that the worst had always already happened. Within this history we will trace the movement of the immanentization of fatalism, a move from a fatalism of transcendence to a fatalism of immanence that will turn out to be at the same time a fatalism of an immanence that is self-transcending, or whose very immanence cannot be distinguished from self-transcendence. This movement will lead us from a fatalism with regard to the absolute to an absolute fatalism; it will move from theology to different philosophical accounts of fatalism that will find their climax in Hegel; and, after everything has ended, it will turn to psychoanalysis, which makes things, again, even worse. The structure of the book thereby also mimics what Hegel in his *Science of Logic* calls "quadruplicity": we do not have only three steps in a dialectical unfolding (Luther, Descartes, Kant) because for a full development we also need to count the totality of the steps (Hegel).[23] But since "the negative or the difference is counted as a *duality*," we have to end twice (Freud)—an argument that will itself be developed in the chapter on Hegel. [24] The argumentative style of the book therefore cannot but be consciously redundant or, in other words, somewhat tautological. This is not the case because I aim to bore my readers but because the counterhistory of rationalism I present cannot but repeat the very same argumentative move time and again in new and different forms. This will not only produce an increasing determinateness for how we can conceive of the idea that the worst has always already happened, but its subsequent determinations will also increasingly make the worst even worse. *Hegel* will be presented as *the ultimate de-terminator* with whom there will not even be Nothing left to cling to: we will be left with less than nothing, that is, with absolute fatalism.

What you are about to read is structurally akin to what Hegel called a "speculative proposition" in which, starting from the subject of a sentence, we first move to a predicate that is supposed to determine the former.[25] The subject thereby is assumed to be a stable and passive ground of predication. But when we reach the predicate, we encounter a peculiar effect, namely that "something of the subject" is repeated in the predicate. Although we assumed that by moving on to the predicate we would have left behind the subject as it was, unchanged, with the resurgence of "something of the subject" in the predicate, we are irritatingly thrown back to the subject because we just encountered it again. But with this forced return we have to change what we previously thought of the subject, since it lost its stability, groundedness, and passivity. If we then return once more to the subject (just to check if it is still there), we cannot but notice that it is not where and what we thought (and maybe still think) it is. Therefore we seem to be stuck with the predicate alone. Yet the predicate is nothing but the subject, only in a different way. As a result we find that the movement of thought is thrown around yet impeded at the same time. Ultimately "only this movement itself becomes the object" of thought.[26] This movement itself forms the object of the present book. Hence, in Hegel's sense, it is a speculative book.

This speculative presentation of the counterhistory of rationalism—and thus also of the precondition for a proper concept of freedom—will therefore not entail a history of the concept of fatalism or an attempt to differentiate fatalism and determinism. The term *fatalism* in this book simply designates the assumption that the worst has already happened, and thus it functions as a foil that will allow us to differentiate various articulations of this assumption. But to reconstruct the history of fatalism within rationalism as a history of worsening is impossible without producing a certain comic effect. This effect, however, is not epiphenomenal but essential. Therefore the book will end with an exposition of why fatalism as the only rationally defensible position cannot but be comic fatalism. On its way through the paradigmatic rationalist positions, on its way to defend rationalism in the form of comic fatalism, the present book, then, imitates a conceptual gesture that can be found in the works of Descartes. After he started his search for a stable and certain ground of knowledge and doubted everything that could be doubted—fatalistically doubting that anything will ever be a certain ground for knowledge—Descartes notes the following: "Before starting to rebuild your house, it is not enough simply to pull it down, to make provisions for materials and architects (or else train yourself in architecture), and to have carefully drawn up your plans; you must also provide yourself with some other place where you can live comfortably while building is in progress. Likewise . . . I formed for myself a provisional moral code."[27] The provisional morality that Descartes relied upon assumed the form of a set of slogan-like codes of conduct. The present book, seeking to dismantle the conceptually weak house in which freedom is still declared to reside, proposes at the end of each chapter also a provisional moral rule. These rules do not form a code of ethics but are rules of orientation that can be drawn from the history of rationalism and may offer "the minimal hold of a consistent subjective position."[28]

To end and finally begin: A well-known saying, often attributed to Fredric Jameson, is that people today can more easily imagine the earth being hit by a comet than a radical transformation of the fundamental (sociopolitical, but also economic) coordinates of our daily life. We know that we believe that it is rather a comet coming from the outside than anything happening on the inside that might possibly induce a transformation of the way things are. But, as this saying implies, we act as if we did not know that we know this: that is, we still act as if we hoped for the world to change from within. This book aims to highlight a crucial aspect of the history of rationalism that served as a means to assume the knowledge that one does not know one has. In short, it tries to imagine the very comet that may devastate the earth, not by imagining it as coming from outer space some time in the future but as an event that, although unacknowledged, has already occurred. With such an inversion we may be able to imagine not only other forms of transformation but also another form of freedom. Yet to do so we first have to abolish freedom and embrace catastrophe, disaster, and the apocalypse. This introduction has tried to show what Hegel has often pointed out in his prefaces, namely that prefaces are absolutely useless when it comes to philosophical works, but it is absolutely necessary to demonstrate and comprehend their uselessness to be able to begin with the work itself. To orient the reader in it, my simple suggestion is this: Start by expecting the worst!

1
Protestant Fatalism

Predestination as Emancipation

Well, if I frighten you, we can always go our own ways.
—Denis Diderot, *Jacques the Fatalist*

Predestined, why not?
—Jean-Paul Sartre, *The Words*

I got so much soul in me that I am barely alive.
—Every Time I Die, "Decayin' with the Boys"

Is There a Choice?

In 1525 Luther retaliated. His reply to Erasmus of Rotterdam was so drastic that the latter retorted, "You plunge the whole world into fatal discord."[1] Their dispute concerned the question of free choice. Erasmus was for it, Luther against it. Luther thereby opposed any form of Aristotelianism, since for him Aristotelians derive their concept of justice from a human (ontic) context, where it normatively describes the appropriate way of acting, and transpose it onto the (ontological) doctrine of God. In so doing Aristotelians forget the ontic-ontological difference. They believe that human beings can contribute to their salvation by means of good works because God shares our normative standards (of justice and reason): there is thus continuity between man and God.

Luther countered such Aristotelianism by pointing out that it conflates man and God: it derives an image of God from the image of the human as a free being. For Luther, however, things are precisely the other way around: God works in us even against our will, which is why true faith never begins with free choice but with a forced reorientation of one's life. To believe is not to actualize a human capacity. Rather the origin of belief, as well as its direction, is God. The advent of faith constitutes a fundamental break in one's life and implies that one quits relying on good reasons and normative or objective capacities. Faith begins "only where the illusion of a remote 'inner world' is disturbed."[2]

Luther here follows St. Paul. Belief emerges from a conversion experience similar to Paul's on the road to Damascus.[3] There is no inner realm (of freedom) from which faith can emerge. Rather "my 'inner' approaches me radically from 'the outer.'"[4] I experience faith only when I encounter God, and I am thus forced to renew myself. This is why anyone who thinks he is free (in matters of faith) and who believes that his or her freedom is manifested in deliberately decided actions is ultimately an Aristotelian (i.e., a nonbeliever). In true faith one encounters an abyss of despair while traversing the illusion that one has anything (objectively) at one's disposal—one learns to break with the idea of freedom as something one possesses.[5] Nothing guarantees salvation, not even incessant striving for good works. On the contrary, if I presume that my works can influence God's judgment and that there is a common measure between man and God, I end up committing blasphemy. The one who is truly free does not identify freedom with a given capacity, but instead experiences the despair that there is nothing we *can* do to achieve what we do not even know how to properly strive for. This is the precondition for encountering God, an encounter that forces us to believe "where [such an] event happens, a fresh breeze overthrows my life."[6] Faith results from encountering something that I would not have believed to be possible before experiencing it. In other words, we do not have the freedom to start believing in something. Freedom is rather that which becomes absolutely necessary for me, but only after an event of faith. Faith strikes me contingently. It seems to be something ungrounded, solely depending on God's will. It seems to result from an absolute necessity and forces me to believe. I have no power against God's will. Freedom and belief result from an event of grace. Franz Rosenzweig rightly stated that Luther's believer "has neither belief nor unbelief, but both . . . happen to him."[7] Hence there is no free will.

Erasmus, however, was not at all happy with Luther's radicalism, as he considered free will to be the precondition of all religiosity. If we were in the hands of a predestining God, Erasmus argued, mankind would be a mere object: we would be neither responsible nor guilty and could never achieve anything on our own. He therefore vindicated "a certain power of freedom" but also granted that Scripture contains "secret places . . . into which God does not want us to penetrate more deeply." Freedom of the will is one of these places. So, if God wants some things to remain unknown to us until we die or Judgment Day comes, "it is more religious to worship them, being unknown, than to discuss them, being insoluble."[8] Luther therefore generates confusion and disorientation, amorality, and an irreligious attitude. This is why Erasmus tried not to take sides for or against free will, instead playing the role of a neutral referee, taking sides against taking sides (and thus against Luther).

Letting God be . . . (Good)

Erasmus claims that Scripture is ambiguous and can be used both for and against free will. But we should not question its consistency, as otherwise the basis of faith and morality starts to teeter. He proposes to call freedom "a power of the human will by which a man can apply himself to the things which lead to eternal salvation, or turn away from them." Thus freedom is a capacity that has a certain amount of efficacy: neither a great amount nor zero efficacy. Take the question, Why did Adam sin? Because he was able to and because his "will seems . . . to have been corrupted by immoderate love toward his spouse." Immoderation is a sin, and Erasmus's God dislikes it as much as Erasmus does. One should never love anything more than God (which makes God appear quite jealous), as this was Adam's sin. But a moderate reading of Scripture argues that even the immoderation of original sin only "obscured" and did not extinguish free will. It made free will tend toward sin. Yet "by the grace of God, when sin has been forgiven, the will is made free to the extent that . . . even apart from the help of new grace it could attain eternal life . . . so it is possible for man, with the help of divine grace (which always accompanies human effort), to continue in the right, yet not without a tendency to sin, owing to the vestiges of original sin in him."[9] Thus, for Erasmus, original sin contaminates our capacity to act, but we are still able to strive for salvation and to attain it with God's help.

To clarify this point, Erasmus introduces three kinds of laws: the law of nature, of good works, and of faith. The first functions like a (trivialized) categorical imperative. It "declares it to be a crime if anyone does to another what he would not wish done to himself." The second issues commands and sanctions that exceed our power but can be met with the help of God. The law of faith commands impossible things, but "because grace is plentifully added to it, not only does it make things easy which of themselves are impossible," it makes them also "agreeable."[10] This is a gradual exposition of how freedom contributes to salvation: we *can* (law of nature) avoid doing to others what we do not want to be done to us. In the first instance freedom is thus a capacity to avoid doing certain things. Second, we *ought* also to strive to follow God's commandments (law of good works), even if such works exceed our capacity. Freedom thus comes with an insight into one's limitations. Third, with divine help (law of faith) we *can* do what we are by nature incapable of doing. But striving for good works is not futile. It is a precondition of salvation. This is *human-divine cooperationism*.

At any rate we have the capacity to follow natural law only because divine grace has already intervened after original sin and (almost fully) reconstituted our capacity. The law of faith is always already in effect. It "always accompanies human effort" and therefore (logically) precedes the law of nature. The law of faith is the invisible bracket written around the set of three laws. And God therein is the unmoved mover, who out of mercy enables us to circle around him. Mankind therefore stands in a continuous relation with God: we are always already indebted to God, without whom we could do nothing. But God must be thought of as separated from all the evil we perform. Evil is a misuse of the capacity given to us by God's mercy, but he himself is eternally good. For Erasmus God's goodness is linked to four kinds of grace: (1) grace that is granted naturally (free will as *natural capacity*); (2) grace that has an extraordinary status (*operative grace*) and provides an occasion to change one's life; (3) grace that emerges when the offer (of operative grace) is accepted (*cooperative grace*); and (4) grace that is linked to achieving one's goal (*truly cooperative grace*). In short, our natural constitution entails the capacity (natural grace) to accept an invitation (operative grace) to effectively strive to perform good works that we are otherwise incapable of (cooperative grace) but can realize with God's help (truly cooperative grace). Human nature was equipped by God to work with him if he reaches out to us. This is why "no sinner ought ever to be secure . . . [and] none ought despair."[11] If there were no free will, we could not work toward receiving God's mercy. Without freedom the whole religious realm would collapse: with no grace, responsibility, sin, and commandments, God would simply be playing dirty games with us. One can thus see that the debate between Erasmus and Luther ultimately revolves around the *proper causality of grace and of freedom.*

This is what is at stake in Luther's doctrine of divine foreknowledge and predestination, which Erasmus therefore had to refute. Erasmus seeks to defend free will without limiting God's power (spoiling his omnipotence), thus conceptually distinguishing divine foreknowledge from predestination. He argues that we know that certain things will happen in the future (say, a solar eclipse), but they do not happen because we know them. The same holds for divine foreknowledge. Erasmus thus introduces a distinction between two types of necessity: antecedent necessity (which predetermines free will) and consequent (after-the-fact) necessity. With consequent necessity one can still account for guilt, sin, merit, and human responsibility tout court. Without it, God's punishments would be "either mad or cruel." He would madly or cruelly throw the powerless sinner, "guilty of nothing . . . into eternal fire."[12] God would not be good; he would be a sadist. Mankind would be his nasty object, and the world would be nothing but one gigantic stage for a sadistic play that cannot even turn into a proper tragedy. A good God punishes only someone who deliberately violates the law of nature or of good works and may even hate him in advance. (God foresees the criminal eclipse the way we foresee the solar one.)

For Erasmus, however, it is crucial to emphasize that we are not just mere puppets in God's predetermining hands. We are, as he argues with Aristotle, God's servants. When servants obey their master, they are active and their works are their own. Just like them, we are the cause of our good works, even though they depend on God's grace. (He refers to instances in which people say, for example, God gave me lovely children, etc.) Erasmus explains the causality of human action as follows: First there is thinking, then willing, and finally doing. There is no free will in thinking and doing (both are caused by God's grace), but a deliberate act of will (consent of the agent) necessarily mediates thought with action. God is thereby the main cause of an action, even if free will is a necessary secondary cause: a causal cooperation leaving room for freedom. This is why for Erasmus a true believer is able to accomplish some things while nevertheless ascribing everything to God, his master and guide. Human nature entails the capacity of free will, but humans are never the sole authors of their actions since their nature depends on God. Based on this complication, Erasmus develops an ontological claim about the nature of all things: Everything has a beginning, a progression, and an end. The first and the last fully depend on God. The capacity to will originates in God's grace, and we can cultivate this capacity if we consent to cooperate with him. He has always already reached out to us. God is a supportive and supporting cooperation partner in matters of human salvation, an "advisor and helper, just as an architect helps his assistant . . . shows him the why and wherefore. . . . What the architect is to his pupil, grace is to our will." Thus "there is nothing that man cannot do with the help of the grace of God."[13]

God is a good, charming architect who enjoys helping and advising. So how do we make sense of those parts of the Scripture that suggest otherwise? In reading them "we are forced willy-nilly to seek some moderation of our opinion." So again, when there seems to be a contradiction in Scripture, or it contradicts our idea of God, there is a simple solution: "We shall be ordered to adore that which is not right to pursue." Moderate interpretation is needed when the consequences of the letter might become a threat to belief, otherwise one cannot avoid "absurd . . . consequences."[14]

To adore what we cannot comprehend is crucial, yet what also "is to be avoided" is to "overthrow free choice, for if this is done away with I do not see any way in which the problem of the righteousness and the mercy of God is to be explained." By claiming that there is no freedom and only "absolute necessity," as Luther argues, we "ascribe cruelty and injustice to God, a sentiment offensive to pious ears (for he would not be God if there were found in him any blemish or imperfection)." For Erasmus evil has to remain external to the notion of God. When man is considered to be incapable of something, God becomes cruel and imperfect, since he is the one responsible for evil. In other words, from Luther's perspective, Erasmus's God is dead. There is only a cruel supreme sadist issuing commandments that are impossible to fulfill by a human nature so weak that it can achieve nothing on its own. For Erasmus this "immeasurabl[y] exaggerate[d] original sin" implies an "excess of zeal" and "a delight in . . . extravagant statements." And it is from "such exaggerated views that have been born the thunders and lightnings which now shake the world," "paradoxes on account of which the Christian world is now in an uproar"—an obvious reference to the peasant revolts of the time.[15] Luther is excessive, extravagant, and he exaggerates. He brings conflict, despair, and fatalism to the entire human race. He is an inhumanist, defending a "pessimistic anthropology" (so the entire issue of humanism is at stake here) with an "apocalyptic perspective."[16] To oppose this extreme position, according to Erasmus, we need moderation, reasonable interpretation, and a humanist theory of cooperation. The fate of the (Christian) world depends on this.

Exaggerating Exaggeration, or
Letting (God) Be . . . (God)

Erasmus's position follows the implicit imperative "Let God be good!" Luther opposes it with his own: "Let God be God!"[17] If Erasmus argues that Luther exaggerates, one should here recall what Adorno once claimed about psychoanalysis: "In psycho-analysis nothing is true except the exaggerations."[18] The same holds for Luther. It is precisely his exaggerations—his defense of absolute necessity, of predestination, and his radical disidentification of freedom and capacity—that, I will argue, touch on a crucial dimension of a radical concept of freedom. Why? Because the one who exaggerates literally goes beyond a certain limit and produces something excessive.[19] Such an excess is at stake in Luther's exaggerations. I thus take Erasmus's critique as an entry point into Luther's thought. This move is justified because Luther himself contends that Erasmus forced him to exaggerate his previous exaggerations: excessively exaggerating exaggerations. Peculiarly and provocatively Luther suggests that this *redoubled and excessive exaggeration* (maybe even a *meta-exaggeration*) generated greater clarity in articulating his own position.[20] How should we understand this exaggeration without measure, something immeasurably excessive, that ultimately coincides with absolute clarity? In his "Manifesto for Reformation," Luther, the Reformation Hercules, demonstrates the inconsistency of Erasmus's position by demonstrating its necessary yet unintended outcome.[21] He drives Erasmus straight into the arms of Pelagius, who contends that in order to avoid (religious) fatalism one needs the primacy of free will over divine grace.[22] We witness here the practice of absolute necessity. We should thus read Luther as a Hegelian avant la lettre, taking the claims of a position seriously by showing how the assumptions on which it relies lead to the very opposite of what the position wanted to assert.

Against Erasmus, Luther seeks not only to defend *absolute necessity* but also the *absolute clarity* of Scripture. The latter is both internally clear (i.e., noncontradictory) and externally clear (i.e., it can be understood by any true believer). Why should God have given it to us otherwise and in any other form? These two claims are dialectically linked: Scripture is clear, but it can be adequately comprehended only if it is read in the right spirit. It thus demands that the spirit of the reader itself demonstrate internal clarity, in the same way that, for example, St. Paul is "his own best interpreter." If the reader encounters ambiguous parts in the Scripture, that is already a sign that she is not a true believer. Or, in more dialectical terms, anticipating a theoretical maneuver that will later become crucial for Descartes, Scripture can be absolutely clear about something by being paradoxical if the thing itself cannot but appear paradoxical to our understanding. This is also to say: No true belief without clarity of Scripture; no clarity of Scripture without true belief. This conclusion is derived from reading Scripture to the letter. A consequence of this is that the composition of Scripture is absolutely necessary the way it is, and thus one needs to read it with the assumption of absolute necessity, to accept "what God says . . . quite simply at its face value." This is why, for Luther, Erasmus argues like a sophist. He is a "wordy rhetorician," "a fluent orator," bending God's word, introducing allegedly subtle but ultimately worthless distinctions. Erasmus reads Scripture "so that anything might be made of anything."[23] In short, he is a postmodernist avant la lettre and in the pejorative sense of the term.

Luther generally despises the idea that certain things should not be discussed publicly when it comes to matters of faith. He detests "such self-censorship of preachers" and asks, "If it is wrong, why do you [Erasmus] do it?"[24] But the true problem is that "you treat this subject as if it were simply an affair between you and me about the recovery of a sum of money"; this sort of bookkeeping does not work in matters of faith and freedom. Erasmus the bookkeeper wants to prevent turmoil in the world and thereby ultimately demonstrates his ignorance toward true questions of faith. Luther asserts in a proto-Leninist manner, "Even we are not made of stone . . . but when nothing else can be done, we prefer to be battered with temporal tumult, rejoicing in the grace of God, for the sake of the Word of God." To lament upheavals is useless, as they did not originate from debates about Scripture but have "arisen and [are] directed from above, and . . . will not cease till . . . the adversaries of the Word [are] mud of the streets."[25] Not to see this is again a symptom of disbelief. In such interesting times, as the Chinese will much later call times of revolt, true faith is more important than ever.

Only in this way can we be prepared to assert, as Luther does in a proto-Maoist fashion, "that changes of things cannot take place without commotion and tumult, nor indeed without bloodshed" (what is at stake is of course that "the kingdom of the pope, with all its followers, is going to collapse"), and that one is ready "to lose the world rather than God." Luther is not simply endorsing manslaughter. Rather he argues that it is always worth risking bloodshed in matters of faith instead of preaching in a fake-pacifist kind of way whose ultimate outcome is that "all souls should be slaughtered and eternally damned while the world is kept in peace." The uproar in the streets is a symptom of a transformation of faith. It originated from God's will, and his "operations are not childish or bourgeois or human, but divine and exceed human grasp." Here we can already get a sense of Luther's radicalism. Turning against God's will and his predestination, one acts childishly or à la bourgeois or simply humanly, all-too-humanly. In short, we become a bourgeois, a humanist, if we opt for free will as something that humans have as a capacity. This also implies that we cannot avoid speaking the truth and should not care if we offend or upset people. Simply because the truth is the truth. And it is eternal and universal, not limited to geopolitical or historically specific conditions. Its medium is Scripture. Geopolitical and historical settings come with certain (political or legal) constraints, yet "the Word of God" sets mankind "free."[26] This is why Luther is a theorist of the letter.[27]

For him Erasmus is not only a moderate bourgeois politician who seeks to negotiate a peace treaty with the world as it is. Even worse, Erasmus also takes sides for human dogmas and against God, since peace is not a concept applicable to God. Thus Erasmus opts for human, worldly freedom against freedom of and in faith, for unfreedom and against true freedom, because God does not act in accordance with human dogmas. God is not a moderator who corrects our worldly performances, trying to make us his more skillful servants. At the same time, he who believes that he can correct his ways all by himself is for Luther a "hypocrite."[28] The first thing we have to assert is that we are and our fate is to be fundamentally helpless without God.

Only "the elect and the godly will be corrected by the Holy Spirit, while the rest perish uncorrected." One should thus not assume that God has always already reached out to us. An event of grace is rare and exceptional as it defies all the laws of probability. If one believes otherwise, one "retains some self-confidence and does not altogether despair of [one]self, and . . . at least hopes or desires that there may be" a chance of salvation. Without despair there will never be salvation. Luther himself describes this experience as follows: "I myself was offended more than once, and brought to the very depth and abyss of despair, so that I wished I had never been created a man, before I realized how salutary that despair was and how near to grace."[29] Without completely abandoning all hope and despair, there can never be an event of grace. Otherwise one still retains some objective ground, a good reason to believe. But belief is radically nonobjective, and there are never good reasons for it. This is the meaning of the claim that belief originates in an event of grace: in short, no love (of God) without prior despair; no love as long as there is still hope. If I truly despair, I see myself as God sees me, as completely incapacitated and worthless. This is why despair is salutary: it enables one to see oneself from an impossible perspective.

Conversely, and although this sounds tautological, despair also forces us to think what seems impossible, namely that one cannot not despair. Otherwise I would be able to freely decide to love (and believe in God). But the love of God, we could argue, is like all true love. We cannot and do not decide to fall in love. This is why I "fall" in love, even if I can decide to get married afterward. In this sense I do not have access to my innermost motives.[30] Love happens to me—and the precondition for such an event is to get rid of all self-confidence, hope, and desire (to fall in love). Why? Because as long as I desire and hope for it, I consider it to be possible. But—and this is Luther's point—an event of grace (from which love emerges) exceeds human grasp and categories. It can be thought only as something impossible. Or, in simpler terms, it can be thought only after the fact. An event of grace occurs when the *impossible qua impossible* happens. And the true question that emerges here is this: Does the impossible happen necessarily or contingently? This is where predestination enters the scene.

Our first answer to the question might be that salvation as much as love is conceptually linked to an experience of utter passivity ("sheer passive necessity of God's working").[31] Something happens that I am unable to willfully provoke.[32] This experience of passivity is anticipated in the experience of despair and anxiety that arises from the insight that salvation, rightly understood, is impossible. We touch upon this impossible point when we reach the abyss of despair whereby there is a movement of torsion that turns despair into something peculiarly salutary. As Žižek argues, "A true decision/choice . . . presupposes that I assume a passive attitude of 'letting myself be chosen.'"[33] In other words, this point is connected to a proper understanding of what the Marxist tradition would refer to, but would also often misunderstand, in terms of self-criticism. Its result is that any true believer is "anguished at [her] roots."[34] What is this anguish? It is what springs from the impossibility of salvation and from the assumption that there will never be any chance for us to experience God's mercy. But does this not abolish faith? Luther answers no. True faith begins when we come to "believe [God is] merciful when he saves so few and damns so many and to believe him righteous when by his own will he makes us necessarily damnable, so that he seems, according to Erasmus . . . worthy of hatred rather than of love."[35] True faith begins by believing in something that has no objective grounding, by assuming the worst, by experiencing anxiety, and by having the insight that there is nothing we can cling to. Faith begins with loving the one who brought this fate upon us. The first imperative of true belief is thus the following: *Love only someone who makes you anxious!*

But how can we then grapple with the question of why God punishes someone if he himself forced this person to do evil? Here we get Luther's first account of the concept of necessity (and thus draw nearer to the issue of predestination). He distinguishes between necessity (*necessitas immutabilitatis*) and compulsion (*necessitas coactionis*). When someone "without the Spirit of God" wills evil, he does so by his own accord. He is not compelled, although he has no capacity to change the direction in which his will moves. The nature of our will immutably turns toward evil, which is a consequence of original sin. There is a "persistent attraction and drive of the will toward evil." Evil is thereby defined as a turn away from God. This is why there is no free choice, but there is no simple compulsion either. If we emphasize the existence of free will, we do not know what we do: we claim to be free, but this freedom simply enforces our fate and makes us assume that we do not need God. Not only are we not free (in our choices), but the freedom we defend immutably thrives on evil. But why are we unable—say, through the help of the commandments—to resist this tendency and strive for the good (although we need grace to achieve it)? Luther's answer is that by trying to resist its own nature, the will is driven into even worse evil (recall Florville's story) simply because sinful self-confidence and self-righteousness emerge from the assumption that one is able to behave virtuously. The only capacity mankind has is a capacity to do evil, and there is no way to resist it. We are incapable of freely redetermining ourselves (our nature), for in this act we would have to rely on the very capacity that we seek to redetermine: there is a compulsion to repeat evil. This means that freedom as capacity is not freedom; it is rather "in all men the kingdom of Satan." It does not even "cease to be evil under [the] movement of God." It is always already contaminated by the immutability of its nature. But this does not exclude responsibility or sin. Rather, as Luther argues, one is even more responsible for that which one cannot change, which is why God is always already justified and right in condemning us. Luther here anticipates Freud's point that although we do not consciously fabricate our dreams, we are obviously responsible for them. For Luther, God "works evil in us, i.e. by means of us, not through any fault of his." We are just like "a horse that is lame in one or two of its feet," which unless it is cured "goes badly." We should never forget: "God owes us nothing," and he does not "act according to human justice . . . or else ceases to be God."[36]

Affirm and Declare: Predestination!

It is crucial to note that, according to Luther, Erasmus necessarily arrives at the very same conclusions even if he seeks to resist them. He thus unwillingly "proves the most powerful subverter of free choice" because he "talks like . . . free choice itself," and therefore one can see all its inconsistencies and evils manifesting in his discourse. If good works depend on God's cooperation, free will is not free, and everything depends on divine grace. For "what is ineffective power but simply no power at all"? Erasmus misuses language ("you would not call a slave free"); defends what is not more than an "empty name," "a reality . . . only in name," "a mere dialectical fiction"; and asserts what he wants to deny. He "is compelled to speak for us and against" himself when he speaks of the existence of free choice, yet is forced to admit its inexistence. He "obscures the sense" of Scripture, just as he himself claims original sin obscured our free will. And he conflates the name of the thing with the thing itself. The only thing that can be permitted to orient our belief is the Word of God incarnated (the Word became Flesh) in the absolutely clear Scripture. Otherwise men "fabricate whatever they please." Erasmus's fabrication consists of "collating everything and affirming nothing."[37] But faith exists only by affirmation and declaration (*apophasis*), not collation (*diatribe*). There is no faith without taking sides.

A paradox emerges here since Luther takes sides against the capacity to choose freely. This position is nonetheless consistent with his earlier arguments because he fully embraces the idea that we are being compelled to choose. He affirms his own incapacity to do otherwise (a repetition of the infamous "Here I stand. I cannot do otherwise"), and he goes so far as to state, "I frankly confess that even if it were possible I should not wish to have free choice given to me, or to have anything left in my own hands." If free choice exists, we must attribute everything to it, and hence we must turn it into something divine, since "there is no need of grace if there so much good in free choice." In this case there would be only free will, no God, no absolute. If there is God, there is no free will, and everything depends on grace. This is thus one of the necessary and fundamental forced choices that any true belief must accept. In this situation there is no true choice: one cannot but opt against freedom. Erasmus seeks to avoid this conclusion by emphasizing a choice without force. But his moderation leads him to defend "a crippled free choice" that depends on grace. At the same time, however, he also "deifies" this free choice (which Luther points out is given "agency" by Erasmus) because for him everything depends on the consent of free choice (which Erasmus claims to be "capable of applying itself to the things that belong to eternal salvation"). And things get worse with and for Erasmus, as he ultimately seems to rely on the idea that the will tends neither toward good nor evil, which implies a "willing in the absolute," an indifferent will, which is for Luther a fundamentally inconsistent idea.[38]

There is free choice, but only in God, on whom everything depends. Hence there is no freedom of the will for "grace would not be grace if it were earned by works." And as God's will is not caused externally, what he willed must be absolutely necessary and immutable. In other words, "for his will there is no cause." God is the only cause, and there cannot be a cause to the cause, no Other of the Other, to use a Lacanian vocabulary. If his will is immutable and necessary, God has willed what he willed for eternity, "even before the foundation of the world." For this reason his "love . . . and hatred [are] eternal, being prior to the creation of the world." This is why there is predestination. This is also why his commandments cannot be fulfilled by us if he does or did not will it so. They exist for us in order to allow us to have the "undeniable experience of how incapable" we are. The law thus generates knowledge of one's own incapacity and impotence, of "how great weakness there is."[39] Commandments produce knowledge of the fact that there is no free will. Erasmus unwillingly relies on the following logic: If man can do as commanded, he does not need grace; if he cannot, he does not need commandments. Luther counters: He needs commandments to realize that he cannot fulfill them and thereby attains knowledge of his incapacity (as the very attempt to fulfill the commandments, relying on one's presumed free will, is what hinders their fulfillment).

This knowledge is true knowledge because this is what Scripture makes clear (and what makes Scripture clear too). It is knowledge of the impossibility of (attaining) salvation (by one's efforts). This knowledge thus produces salutary despair, and it can itself arise from a faithful reading and experience of Scripture. This knowledge is also knowledge of a difference that differs from all differences that one encounters in the world. It implies the affirmation of the fact that there is no common measure that relates God and mankind—*there is no human-divine relationship*. Erasmus falsely assumes that there is a continuity between man and God and thereby also confuses "God preached and God hidden."[40] It is precisely this distinction (in Hegelian terms, that between God for us and God in itself) that needs to be taken into account. God is *not* his Word. The Word is God revealed to mankind. To think God, one needs to avoid the temptation of fusing revelation (the Word, Christ) and God as such. Fusing them implies that one loses not only the Real (of) God but also revelation, thus failing to see the clarity of Scripture. One therefore needs to resist the temptation to make One out of them (as Erasmus does).

Forgetting this—in Heideggerian terms, ontic-ontological—difference, we start to search for reasons behind God's will. But, as Luther contends, God's will "is no business of ours," which is why we have to stick to that which was revealed to us, namely his Word.[41] Luther's position differs radically from Calvinist doctrine, where one is constantly searching for signs of the status of our salvation and is even driven to produce these signs oneself by being successful in the mundane world, thus reinscribing God's motives into the realm of the at least potentially humanly knowable. This is what one may call the Weberian story of the Reformation. It is often neglected that Weber was aware that this is primarily the nature of Calvinist and not of Lutheran theology—even if the latter provided the former's foundation. Felix Ensslin argues that Luther prevents such a position precisely by means of his doctrine of predestination and his prohibition to speculate about God's motives.[42] Weber himself indicates that this distinction points to a crucial difference between Luther and Calvin. The former emphasized anxiety and despair, whereas for the latter, who "viewed all pure feelings and emotions . . . with suspicion, faith had to be proved by its objective results in order to provide a firm foundation for the *certitudo salutatis*."[43] One can see that from a Lutheran perspective both Erasmus and Calvin are objectivists in matters of faith, and this makes their respective positions untenable.

Luther's position, in contrast, implies that we must renounce all speculations about God's motives. What is impossible— namely to decipher God's motives—is therefore also prohibited. There is a radical gap, a difference different from all other differences, that separates the revealed God (Scripture) and God in himself (the hidden or "naked" God). This split needs to be thought in order not to "measure God by human reason," which would be literally "perverse." From this springs Erasmus's "thoroughly perverse use of language" that is a direct manifestation of this problem and makes him a "perverter of Scripture": Erasmus the pervert.[44]

To avoid perversion we have to insist that we can conceive only of the revealed God. To put it differently, we have to insist on the gap that separates this revealed God from God in himself. God in himself exceeds all human notions and is thus necessarily unthinkable. We can think him (or her) only by exaggeratingly exaggerating to the extent that we clearly comprehend how excessive this excess really is. If "we can do nothing of the things commanded," we discover that his revelation is in excess of our capacities: "Works of God are entirely beyond description." We thereby realize that the hidden part of God must even be in excess of this excess—a meta-excess without measure, hence Luther's excessive rhetoric. We can only "fear and adore" his will since "who are we that we should inquire into the cause of the divine will?" In other, more profane words, the only thing to do with regard to the will of God is to not give a fuck about it. We can relate to his will only as it is revealed to us, which is, in short, "the will of Christ." This is what it means to let God be God. The true believer thus acts with a proto-Kantian "will that is disinterested in seeking any reward . . . being ready to do good even if—an impossible supposition—there were neither kingdom nor hell." True belief implies disinterest in one's own salvation, which has to be considered impossible (to be attained by us) anyhow. True belief puts "a restraint on the rashness of Reason" and prohibits speculating about what is impossible to think in the first place. Untrue belief, in contrast, indulges in "useless speculations and questionings about [our] worthiness," speculations into God's motives and into his rewards for our actions. It thereby understands all action as a means to an end—the reward that results from it: bookkeeping. The opposition to this economism of belief is what motivates the (logical) prohibition to speculate and thus frames Luther's concept of predestination. Letting God be God, however, implies a letting be in another sense as well. We can act in such a manner that we are not the agents of our actions. Not only do we have to let God be God, but we also have to let go with regard to our own actions. This is clearly what offends human reason, which is why it is structurally indistinguishable from "human stupidity." But the elect "see with God's eyes," which means that they also see themselves as God sees them, namely as unworthy, impotent, despairing without him.[45] One has to let go, as one does while laughing—because our condition is ultimately so bad that it becomes laughable, or comic. From the very beginning fatalism and laughter are thus connected.

But all this is to say that faith itself enables one to take this paradoxical perspective on oneself, a perspective that leads to utter despair. This perspective also implies a foreknowledge of everything that will happen. In other words, God knows what will happen, otherwise he could err or be deceived. It should therefore be clear that God can be God only if he is considered omnipotent. But omnipotence does not mean "the potentiality by which he could do many things which he does not, but the active power, by which he potently works all in all." Potential omnipotence would imply that he could intervene in the world but refrains from it. Only actual omnipotence is real omnipotence, and real omnipotence implies that he works in everything in the world. It refers to "the unceasing activity of God in created things." If this is the case, it is clear that his omnipotence also implies that he necessarily does so and that everything is already decided in advance. From this emerges the "painful awareness that we are under necessity," a thesis that cannot avoid fundamentally offending human reason.[46] It is inhuman.

This inhuman thesis, however, offends human reason because reason likes to praise God when he saves the unworthy but dislikes it when God punishes the virtuous. The latter is an offense against the reasonable (and moderate) assumptions of free will, virtue, human responsibility, and justice. In making such assumptions reason just "seeks and praises herself," and reason's advocates, like Erasmus, necessarily "go from bad to worse." We need to embrace our incapacity and lift it to the point of despair, where salvation seems impossible, since it is already "written in the hearts of all alike, that there is no such thing as free choice." So somehow we do know. But we do not know that we know. (This is precisely how Freud defines the unconscious: a knowledge we do not know we have.) Only through despair and the salubrity of faith do we acquire a belief in the existence of this knowledge. Through despair and anxiety we come close to know what we do not know that we know. One needs to embrace the truth that everything is always already lost, that this is our fate. One thus needs to endorse a proper fatalist position, since only in this way can one avoid the move from bad to worse. Only in this way can one affirm that there are no objective guarantees for salvation. Erasmus and human reason—another human capacity—are therefore basically Aristotelian since they assume an objective teleology that is always already at work and can be judged according to human norms. Against this position one needs to affirm the rationality of the irrational. One can begin by affirming that "free choice does many things"—like "eating, drinking begetting, ruling"—"but that these are nonetheless 'nothing' in the sight of God," a sight that we can attain when we truly despairingly believe. But when we lose sight of this, we assume human-divine cooperation, a "division of labor," which makes faith into a gigantic capitalist enterprise, with God as its charming, moderating boss (who even invites you for a drink from time to time and with whom you work as well as play squash).[47]

For Luther, in order to avoid capitalizing (on) faith, as the church of Luther's time was already doing, we need "to prepare ourselves for the new creation of Spirit," for a "new birth . . . or renewal, regeneration," for a "transformation of the old man" "born anew from God." This preparation—which "excludes preparations for grace" and is thus a preparation without preparation—needs to start by assuming what man wanted before the first creation, namely nothing, because he did not exist. Man "neither does nor attempts to do anything toward becoming a creature." Preparing to become "a new creature of the Kingdom of Spirit," "a being created anew through faith," we also need to assume that God will do it "without us" being actively involved. The only possible preparation lies in the assumption that there will never be any salvation whatsoever. Thus there is no preparation since "if grace comes from . . . the predestination of God, it comes by necessity and not by our own effort."[48] There is predestination, and this means that we have no influence on our fate. Salvation (if it is not graciously granted) is impossible, for nothing is in our power.

Religion as Capitalism versus Subtractive Theology

Erasmus seeks the kind of objective knowledge of God that would make both God and human being appear to be good. This knowledge is supposed to ensure human responsibility, which must be grounded in a capacity, namely free will as something that belongs to human nature. But he thereby avoids taking the mysteries for what they are: mysteries. For Erasmus we somehow already know what we need to know, and we can rely on the objective fact that God is good and we are free. We can work for our salvation and obtain it through good works. Erasmus thus proposes that our task is to cultivate a given objective capacity. Yes, this capacity does tend toward evil, but with discipline (and punishment) it can be made into a cooperative capacity that helps us attain salvation. Everyone should hope—or even assume—that she will be saved if she works for salvation and uses her chances successfully. Grace is always possible, and only those are guilty who do not cultivate this capacity or apply it unsuccessfully. Erasmus's theory is thus not only fundamentally

Aristotelian (defending freedom as a capacity and the idea of its teleological realization) and cooperationist, but it is also a story of human success, not of the American but of the human dream: this is how we move through cooperation from the sinning dishwasher to the saved millionaire. This is not capitalism as religion, but religion as capitalism.

Luther, on the other hand, holds that "my salvation is out of my hand"; that there is no chance of salvation; that all hope is futile; that I have nothing in my power (against this truth); and that only God's exceptional grace may, if he so predestined it, save me.[49] His *subtractive theology* opposes not only a wrong exceptionalism ("All are guilty that do not . . .") but also a wrong universalism (i.e., an objective one: "Everyone may have the opportunity to . . ."). Rejecting these misconceptions, he contends that *not-all are condemned* because God elects some of them through elections that from our perspective are necessarily contingent. Election is when the impossible happens *as* impossible. This implies that one must deny free will and learn not to will—not even to will nothing. The necessity to affirm God's predestination implies also that one must *learn through faith how to inexist*. As this is how one prepares (without being able to) for being reborn—considering oneself as not yet being created, always already noncreated. How to will not to be, thus how to let go, let be. We can clearly see here how Luther's universalism asserts that anyone can be struck by the impossible event of God's grace. It is thus necessary to have faith but impossible to do so, as it can be brought about only by God, and there is no relation between God and mankind. Famously Luther gave one of the most inhuman, charming definitions of the human being as a piece of shit that fell out of God's anus. Mankind has an excremental status. The world is but a gigantic latrine. It was only Calvin's competitive religion that before long would seek to turn this view of the world into a success story by reintroducing constant speculations about God's will and the status of one's own salvation. In Luther's *subtractive and inhumanist theology* one confronts the necessary and yet impossible status of faith. Against any trivializations of God's decisions, against any attempt to mine meaning out of them, Luther defends the knowledge that something unknowable, unthinkable is at work within us. His theology thus affirms a knowledge that we do not know that we have as the basis of faith, namely the knowledge about our excremental status. His claim is that this can happen only through faith alone. In making this claim he not only defends the inhuman kernel of human being but also comes very close to taking up a peculiar Kantian position avant la lettre: limiting reason to make room for faith. But he also delineates the proper rationalist framework for thinking that which we cannot think, namely God in himself, since this thought would be nothing but a "shock for our cognition."[50] He thereby emphasizes the liberation from the idea that freedom is a capacity. The first maxim of a rationalist provisional morality is thus the following: *Act as if you did not exist!*

2
René the Fatalist

Abolishing (Aristotelian) Freedom

*Everybody knows that your orders are like wind in a chimney
until they've been confirmed by Jacques.*
—Denis Diderot, *Jacques the Fatalist*

*Yet all depends upon his providence, to which . . . I submit myself
with as much courage as Father Joseph would have done.*
—René Descartes, "Letter to Mersenne (9 January 1639)"

We did not understand Descartes.
—Stéphane Mallarmé, "Notes sur le langage (1869)"

We need to kill Aristotle!
—Alain Badiou, "Event and Truth"

Desire (Differently)!

In 1649, almost 125 years after Luther opposed Erasmus by contending that there is no relation between man and God and
defended the idea that true faith must begin by accepting the
divine and unknowable doctrine of predestination, Descartes
published his last book. Descartes, "with [whom] the new epoch
in Philosophy begins, whereby it was permitted to culture to
grasp in the form of universality the principle of its higher spirit
in thought," and with whom philosophy experiences "a radical

new beginning," published a book at the end of his life that seems to have anticipated the end of his thought.[1] Today this book, *The Passions of the Soul*, is usually considered to be of merely historical significance, a philosophical nonentity of little importance to any understanding of Descartes's thought. The book was ridiculed because it posited a material link between the two substances that Descartes distinguished in his preceding work: the body and the soul.[2] This link served as the material interface of their mediation, the seat of the soul in the body— the infamous pineal gland.[3] It may be due to the book's alleged obsoleteness, or to the efficacy of the harsh critiques it received, that some of its most astonishing arguments went unnoticed: arguments suggesting that Descartes—who was attacked by Dutch Calvinists for being an atheist—was ultimately a fatalist, a strict defender of divine providence.

Descartes and fatalism? It helps to first clarify the topic of his last book. Sartre once stated the obvious: the book deals with the fact that the "Cartesian will is free, but there are 'passions of the soul.'"[4] *The Passions of the Soul* is a book on freedom— understood as freedom of the will—under the conditions of its embodiment. Thus it examines the effects this very embodiment has on freedom and asks what impedes and hinders freedom. As it turns out, and this may come as a surprise, for Descartes passions are freedom's primary obstacle. If the soul is "principally considered as something that wills," the will can suffer from passions that inhibit the realization of its own freedom.[5] As Descartes states, "Of all kinds of thoughts which the soul may have, there are none that agitate and disturb it so strongly as the passions."[6] In short, because of the passions, the will can make use of itself poorly. This means that the soul has two distinct kinds of attributes: actions and passions. The actions of the soul (its volitions) are caused by the soul, and they can be directed either toward the soul or toward the body—say, when one wants to stand up and the body starts to move. The passions of the soul are basically perceptions that originate in the body or in objects outside of us so they first affect us through our senses. But they have an effect on the body as well as the soul. Yet things get more complicated. Not only do passions appear in the soul as volitions (they move the soul to will something, say, an external object), but volitions that originated in the soul also generate passions (for example, joy about an amazing idea). Volitions can lead to passions (what Descartes calls "internal emotions"), but passions can likewise lead to volitions.

Externally generated passions represent something that did not originate in the soul but is nonetheless represented within the soul as if it originated in the soul. These passions do not simply overwhelm and determine the soul. Even if weakened and disoriented in its self-determining power, the soul still remains the determining subject of all its actions due to the simple fact that the soul essentially is a substance separable from all external objects, including the body. Although the soul is never abolished as substance by its passions, misdirected actions can occur as a result of the passions' influence on the self-determination of the soul (i.e., of the will). The soul then takes the representation of a volition that is caused by an external object as if it were caused by the soul itself. But even then the formal structure of the will remains intact, even if the will wills something that is in contradiction to its own nature (namely unfreedom). This means that it is possible for one to *freely will unfreedom* when moved by passions. Passions always "represent to us the goods to whose pursuit they impel us as being much greater than they really are."[7] They are exaggerated representations that seduce us to follow their lead. This is possible precisely because passions are represented as volitions of and within the soul. And thus they move the soul and may solicit actions. In short, passions generate desire.[8]

This desire, however, is not caused by the soul itself. It may appear as if it were a product of free self-determination, but it lacks freedom. Thus in order to avoid following a desire that obeys an external form of causality that one does not recognize as what it is (i.e., to not simply follow the solicitations of the body but to act as an embodied free being), the soul has to struggle "with these representations, aiming at instituting other associations than those formed by nature or habit."[9] The task for Descartes is thus to *change the operativity of desire*. The first thing that needs to be established is the distinction between different kinds of passions: on the one hand, we have desire that did not originate in the soul; on the other, we have volitions that originated in the soul and thus have the causality of freedom. (Descartes also speaks of self-causation.) Pierre Guenancia rightly infers from this that "the freedom of the soul is nothing but this possibility of instituting other links and consequently other actions than those of which the body disposes, or the institution of nature or habit."[10] Descartes thus situates the causality of freedom in a place where there is a different way of relating to the order of externally caused desire. Freedom emerges when the natural (bodily) and habitual (second-order natural) causal order and its effects on the soul are determined in a new way. Thus Descartes does not simply advocate the peculiar fantasy of liberating oneself from one's own body and from the order of nature or habit altogether; rather what he seeks to demonstrate is that freedom consists in establishing a *different mode of desire*.

This understanding of freedom, however, does not lead to a rejection of representations in general. Rather Descartes locates freedom in a new way of relating to representations, which initially means that the distinction between the order of nature and the order of freedom can be retained. Once again Descartes emphasizes his famous methodological idea that the right practice of cognition arises from clarity and distinction, with the latter being the more important source. The distinction between self-caused volitions (causality of freedom) and externally caused passions (mechanical causality of nature) is important for the proper conception of freedom. But this conceptual line of demarcation does not mean that freedom is simply the opposite of the passions. Rather the question is how to deal with a perception of an external thing that is represented as volition within the soul, that is, as something that moves the soul to strive to attain it. This means that passions do "not constitute the sense of an object, but a proper and internal way of the soul to react to the action of certain objects."[11] Freedom consists in a different use of the passions, a new way of modeling and understanding their representational structure, and a different mode of determining the actions that result from it. For this reason, Descartes claims "that persons whom the passions can move most deeply are capable of enjoying the sweetest pleasures of this life. It is true that they may also experience the most bitterness when they do not know how to put these passions to good use. . . . But the chief use of wisdom lies in its teaching us to be masters of our passions and to control them with such skill that the evils which they cause are quite bearable, and even become a source of joy." *Freedom is a different use of the desire that the passions create. It enables the subject to desire something that would otherwise be impossible to desire.*[12] This can even turn unbearable evils into a source of joy.

This new use of desire (and thus passions) introduces a difference into the given, mechanical, natural order of passions such that they can be known, understood, judged properly, and dealt with in a practice that relies on the primacy of self-determined actions of free will. Without the distinction between the causality of freedom and the causality of nature, and without willing to act according to this distinction, an action of free will could result from a mechanical, or externally imposed, cause and end up being a form of external unfreedom.[13] As Descartes indicated in his "Conversation with Burman," however, the problem should not be located within the being of the free will itself but rather in the way the will and the understanding interact with regard to the passions. In other words, the question concerns the way judgments based upon our knowledge of passions and their difference with regard to volitions make it possible to continue to will freely. This means that heteronomously determined (or naturally caused) actions do not "show any imperfection in our will, merely inconstancy in our use of it. Each act of the will is as perfect as the next: the fluctuation you [Burman] speak of comes from our judgment; it happens we don't judge well. . . . The imperfections that beset our judgment come from intellectual ignorance. If this were removed, the fluctuation would disappear along with it, and our judgment would be stable and perfect." Descartes adds that "sins arise from ignorance, no-one can pursue evil *qua* evil . . . our will is corrupted by emotions."[14] Sins are the result of ignorance and lack of understanding (i.e., lack of judgment). No thinking being could will evil if it knew that it were evil and had a proper concept of it, since this would be self-contradictory and violate the very laws of reason. Evil is a secondary, privative state, and evil deeds are privative actions since they manifest the lack of knowledge of what a proper action is. But evil can arise out of our passions.

When we expand our will onto something that is unknown to us, our passions are fundamentally obscure and opaque to us because we are unable to distinguish them from true volitions that originated in the soul rather than elsewhere. To be guided by passions therefore means to be guided by ignorance or partial knowledge and leads to vacillation in judgment. In contrast, certain, clear, and distinct knowledge may produce firm judgments, which are the will's "'proper' weapons" and hence produce true actions, in which the action itself is imbued with the self-determination of the will through and through. The crucial way of making different use of our passions thus springs from being able to judge them as what they are on the basis of sufficient knowledge. This knowledge and adequate judgment thus cannot but rely on the clear distinction between movement that is immanently caused in the soul and movement that is caused externally. If there is insufficient knowledge or none at all, then there is an instability in one's judgments. In addition this state also characterizes "the weakest souls of all . . . whose will is not determined . . . to follow such judgments, but constantly allows itself to be carried away by present passions."[15] The weakest souls vacillate in their judgments because they take passions for volitions and get confused due to a lack of proper understanding of the distinction between passion and volition.

Becoming a Movement

What complicates this conclusion is that there are also self-caused passions. Descartes calls them "internal emotions" that "are produced in the soul only by the soul itself." Internal emotions are generated when what the will judges to be good coincides with the volition directed toward this good. Therefore if one's volition moves the soul to do good, the result is a specific internal emotion: joy.[16] Something originating within the soul moves it, and the soul judges this movement to be joyful and desirable. The perception of one's own voluntary movement combined with a judgment of that movement as desirable generates pleasure or joy. Through internal emotions, the soul senses itself to be free in the very act of being moved. In a passionately agitated state, in contrast, the soul senses movement but remains confused about the origin of this movement. Internal emotions make the soul sense that its own movement is realizing its own freedom, which is why the soul strives to perpetuate this very movement. The move from passion to internal emotion is thus the move from one natural order of causation (in which the soul is moved like an object by the effect another object has on it) to another one: from being moved to being the cause of movement; from being moved by the effect of a represented object to the *becoming indistinguishable of the subject and the object of movement*; from being moved by an external force that makes one desire a specific action to seeking to remain within the movement and continue desiring, whereby *movement and immobility within this movement become indistinguishable* in the form of a compulsion to repeat the movement. This is a move from natural causality to the causality of freedom, which changes the very mode of movement. The latter ultimately consists in *becoming the movement* that actualizes itself *hic et nunc* and realizes in every act the infinity of the will's freedom.

This new movement effectively amounts to a *becoming indistinguishable between the thing and its representation, between presentation and representation*—"an indistinguishable mixture of idea and thing."[17] Moving from externally caused passions to internal ideas, one does not abolish passions because within this move internal emotions occur. Rather one is able to judge properly because the will can freely judge only that which is clear and distinct. In this move, passions and volitions become distinguishable, which enables clarity because what is most clear to the will is what originates in the soul itself. Here one can see a move from passionate representation, that is, from how passions "appear" within the soul, to the *being of representation*, which makes it possible to understand their nature and enables the will to produce within the soul a judgment about the will's proper volition by discriminating passions from volitions. The soul thereby returns to itself. Since the "being" of representation *is* the soul, even the passions would have no existence within the soul without the soul. In this return of the soul to itself, the will makes itself into its own object. It thus relates to itself in such a way that it is moved by itself.

Because *The Passions of the Soul* deals with the union of body and soul, the move from representations within the soul (passions) to the being of representation (which is the soul) enables us to distinguish between two forms of practice: "There is . . . a great difference between the resolutions which proceed from false opinion and those which are based solely on knowledge of the truth. For, anyone who follows the latter is assured of never regretting or repenting."[18] Only by knowing the truth about passions and distinguishing them from volitions can we act in such a manner that we will never have to regret our decisions. In the case of true actions of freedom, the soul will never have anything to regret even if they lead to the worst outcomes, as these actions did not have any other cause but the soul itself. This is a practice subtracted from revoking and repenting, a practice of firm decisions (judgments). In short, a *practice of truth*. But if what is at stake in Descartes's *Passions of the Soul* is the positioning of an active practice of truth (and internal emotions) against a reactive practice of passions, possible regret, revocation, instability, and revisability, the question appears even more pressing: How can we reconcile this practice of truth with the defense of fatalism?

Desiring Fortune

Descartes mentions fatalism twice in *The Passions of the Soul*. The term first appears in article 145 in the second part of the book, which deals with "those desires which depend solely on other causes; and what Fortune is." It appears again in the subsequent article, which discusses "those desires which depend on us and on others." The book as a whole is divided into three parts. The first part deals with the general nature of the passions against the background of the theory of free will and demonstrates the separate nature of the body and the soul. The second part deals with the logical order of the most fundamental passions (wonder, love, hate, sadness, joy, and desire). The third part examines the possible composites of these fundamental passions. Fatalism comes up in the context of the fundamental passions close to the end of the second part. To be precise, fatalism appears just before Descartes introduces the "internal emotions" of the soul related to the practice of truth and freedom and claims that "the exercise of virtue is a supreme remedy against the passions."[19] Fatalism therefore arises as the mediating link between a practice of passions and the practice of freedom. It makes possible the move from one form of practice to the other.

The title of article 145 ("Those desires which depend solely on other causes; and what Fortune is") already makes it clear that Descartes is dealing with things that depend on causes outside of us. He begins by stating that one should not passionately desire that which does not depend on our will. This statement implies that things depending solely on us we cannot "desire too much; it is rather that we desire too little." We cannot desire things that depend on us too much, yet for things that do not, even a little desire seems too much, "however good they may be." Things independent from us should not be desired, but not simply because the desired event may not be realized (like not winning the lottery), which in turn may afflict us. Rather it is because desiring them deflects our attention from the things that actually do depend on us. In desiring things that are not in our power, we do not will what we can self-determinately will. We thereby will to be determined heteronomously. The will wills without freely determining what it wills. And the external things that the will wills "occupy . . . our thoughts," overwrite all other thoughts, and absorb us.[20] Hence the will also wills without determining how it wills. The passions that solicit us to desire such things thereby misdirect our will and corrupt our thoughts. As a consequence of this corruption, in the very act of what it perceives as volition (passionate desire), the will is *turned inside out* (as it is occupied with things external to and beyond its power) because it has fully *internalized its outside* (and moves from self-determination to heteronomous determination). In this very manner the will still wills, but what and how the will wills is not determined and hence not willed by itself. As a consequence of willing and not-willing, self-determination and heteronomous determination become indistinguishable for the will itself. The will wills, but it loses track of the fact that in a strict sense it does not will but is moved by something coming from the outside. The will wills as if it willed, but it does not truly (i.e., freely) will anymore. Due to this structure of desire, *the will acts as if it were free, yet it is not.*

If the will does not freely determine what and how it wills, it is moved by something outside of it (that appears to the will as if it were something it willed freely, since it nonetheless has to will it). The ultimate result of this is that now the soul—whose medium is the will—behaves as if it were a body that is moved by another body. This is because for Descartes movement and rest are modes of the body and depend on the relations to other bodies.[21] By desiring things that are beyond the scope of the will, the will cannot practically materialize its freedom. Hence what Descartes tries to tackle is the *practice of unfreedom*. Martial Guéroult's observation apropos Descartes's cogito argument is quite instructive here: "'I think that I exist and I know that I know, because I am thinking that I think, but if I were to stop thinking that I think, ought I not inevitably stop thinking that I exist, stop knowing that I know, and consequently stop being certain?' And inevitably I stop thinking that I think when . . . I turn my thought away from myself in order to fix it on another thing."[22] To translate this interpretation into the terms of our own discussion, we could say that I freely will to be free, and

I know that I know, because I am freely willing that I will. But if I were to stop freely willing that I will, ought I not inevitably stop freely willing to be free, stop knowing that I know, and consequently stop acting freely? And, inevitably, I stop freely willing my freedom when I turn my will away from myself in order to desire a thing independent of my will. But because I still perceive my own volitions as free volitions and do not know that I am determined by things outside myself, I lose the capacity to distinguish between externally caused passions and self-caused volitions. In a proto-Marxist manner, the conclusion can be summed up as: *I do not know that I am not willing freely (I do not know what I do), but I nonetheless do it.*

To counter the confusion of not-willing freedom and will-ing freedom, Descartes introduces two conceptual strategies: "There are two general remedies for such vain desires. The first is generosity" and "the second is frequent reflection upon divine Providence: we should reflect upon the fact that nothing can possibly happen other than as Providence has determined from all eternity. Providence is, so to speak, a fate [*une fatalité*] or immutable necessity, which we must set against Fortune in order to expose the latter as a chimera which solely arises from an error of our intellect."[23] This passage clarifies that Descartes's fatalism cannot simply be reduced to a mechanistic determinism, since this would make us regress to the causality of nature and the body, which is precisely what needs to be avoided. Rather this fatalism is characterized as a belief in divine providence and immutable necessity. Fatalism for the first modern philosopher comes down to a defense of predestination that can be linked conceptually to Luther's defense of absolute necessity. At first sight Descartes's claim may seem to be paradoxical. If we seek to avoid external determination, how can the remedy lie in assuming that everything is determined by God's providence, that is, by something that exceeds the scope and influence of my will and thus appears to be another external determination? How can we resolve this contradiction?

First, one should remark that the contradiction occurs only when one reads this line of argument as a simple replacement of one external cause with another. But Descartes's argument is more specific, as he opposes a fatalist belief in providence to "an error of our intellect that goes under the name 'Fortune.'"[24] We rely on this error as soon as we desire things that do not depend on us because of two implications of the concept of fortune. First, fortune has a cognitive implication. Believing in fortune, I emphasize the possibility or "may-being" of things that are out of my hands. I may win the lottery, and I may not. I do not have the knowledge of how things may go, which is one of the reasons they are out of my hands. The outcome depends on causes external to that of my own will, causes of which I do not know enough. Therefore attaining knowledge about the outcome—this is the second implication—depends on time, more precisely on the future. The future will show if my desire for the millions I can win in the lottery will be satisfied. This conceptual concatenation turns the future into something that I cannot predict in advance and that is therefore beyond the scope of my action and will.

One problem arises at this point, namely that I thereby attain a weak, and therefore problematic, concept of contingency. If things can go either way but the choice is not mine, I identify contingency with arbitrariness, such that the future outcomes of choices depend on good or bad luck. As soon as I do so, my will is determined neither by knowledge nor by the rigidity of its judgments but by arbitrariness. Descartes in this moment anticipates Hegel, who states that arbitrariness is the "will as contradiction."[25] By desiring things independent from myself, my will is heteronomously determined by an arbitrary future outcome. But a will that is determined arbitrarily is not free in its actions. As a result we can read the defense of immutable necessity as a step to overcome this problematic concept of contingency (as arbitrariness) that determines my will and with it the state of unfreedom that results from it. This defense, therefore, does not work simply by playing out one externality against another but by emphasizing necessity against contingency for the sake of unfolding a strong concept of contingency, as will be demonstrated below. In order to achieve this goal, we have to shift our temporal focus from the future to an already determined and yet still determining past, a shift that is performed by way of an appeal to divine providence. Cartesian fatalism thus counters the idea of arbitrary future outcomes that determine the will with the assumption of an always already necessarily determined past (and thereby a fully determined future).

The belief in and reliance on fortune is connected to passions that emerge only when one believes in fortune (otherwise they do not emerge), namely hope (if "there is much . . . prospect of our getting what we desire") and fear (if there is little prospect): "Thus we may hope and fear, even though the expected outcome does not depend on us at all."[26] Hope and fear belong together, for "what, in fact, is hope if not a sort of fear with its head hidden?"[27] We fear and hope in relation to the arbitrary future outcome of externally desired things. Consequently these passions not only are related to the future but also start to determine our present conduct. In short, desiring external and independent things leads to the fact that one does not properly act and live in the present anymore. *The present is lost*, which means that we can experience neither joy nor sadness proper, since only the "consideration of a present good arouses joy in us and consideration of a present evil arouses sadness."[28] If the satisfaction of our desires relies on good or bad fortune, we do not only hope and fear but by doing so we are also *here and now* unable to relate to the present.

By depending on fortune we hypostatize a future that takes over the present. Desire takes over our thoughts, which now solely focus on the future. This, in turn, eliminates the present of thought (and of free will). This way we always already live in our future and abolish our present.[29] In more precise terms, we can claim that even the concept of the future, as the time in which the arbitrary outcome of things will become manifest, is a weak one. It somehow "annihilates . . . the future. Not . . . some abstract future, but the future of the very present, the future of its proper present."[30] When desiring external things, not only is the will not truly present as what it is (as something free), but it also believes that only the future is worth desiring and that thoughts about the past are meaningless. Even worse, through the very act of desiring the future the will abolishes its own present as well as the very future of this present. Time collapses, as it is emptied out of its dimensions. Desiring external things that depend on fortune is literally time-consuming. What Cartesian fatalism opposes is therefore this problematic conception of externality, of contingency, of action, and ultimately of temporality. Fatalism opposes hope just as much as it opposes fear, since they inevitably lead to these problematic consequences.

Cartesian fatalism rejects this inconsistent, obscure idea of the aims, ends, and means of human conduct. It thereby formulates the *preconditions for a proper practice of truth and freedom*; for a *true understanding of time* that works by restoring the present of the free will through an affirmation of a determinate past; and for a *proper conception of contingency* through a defense of necessity. But how does something that at first seems to be the abolition of freedom become a precondition for truly free conduct? Deborah J. Brown rightly remarks, "The rejection of fortune or lack as necessary condition for virtue and the good life . . . represented something of a trend against the powerful figure of Aristotle. Those who rejected the existence of fortune could not ... embrace Aristotle's eudemonistic ethics, in which happiness, the exercise of virtue in a complete life, depended upon some degree of good fortune."[31] What is at stake here for Descartes is thus an opposition to any Aristotelian form of ethics. Aristotelianism is attacked for necessarily inscribing fortune into all realizations of freedom.

A brief detour through Hegel can help clarify this point. Hegel also criticizes eudemonistic ethics, which starts from the idea that the human condition entails a mixture of freedom and unfreedom (soul and body, so to speak), and that this very mixture, ultimately embodied in the natural drives, is what defines the category of arbitrariness. (The will can arbitrarily will freedom or unfreedom.) The drives guide the will to certain ends and are therefore positive. Yet they are also negative because each drive, conceptually understood, excludes all others. From this positive direction and negative exclusiveness, the idea emerges that one can create a whole out of the particular drives, in which they would all be reconciled with one another. This is for Hegel the eudemonistic "idea of bliss."[32] But this idea of the satisfaction of all the drives within a harmonious whole still remains fundamentally determined by the natural function of the drives. The concept of bliss is thereby derived from the natural determination that is already at work within the drives, although on a seemingly higher level. Thus Aristotelian eudemonistic ethics turns out to be an ethics based on the universalization of natural determinations—one reason Aristotelians use the concept of the "life-form." Yet for Hegel natural determinations are not freely posited since they constitute a form of external determination even though they may be internally external. From this perspective, Aristotelianism generalizes the idea of external causality and thus is conceptually forced to endorse the category of fortune. Aristotelianism understood in this way expands an idea of (external) natural determination into the realm of human action and freedom and thereby necessarily naturalizes it.

Applying Hegel's point to Descartes's argument, we could say that Aristotelian ethics and its category of fortune must be rejected because they are based on the generalization of natural causality. As a result they naturalize human nature, which leads to the one-sided hypostatization of the natural part of the human being: the body. This naturalization thus defines human nature in reference to naturally given capacities. Aristotelian ethics therefore naturalizes freedom and the whole realm of free actions. Consequently it absorbs the very freedom of actions into nature and makes them dependent on the future outcomes of things that we cannot influence. For Descartes, Aristotelianism implies naturalization insofar as it makes my will and freedom dependent on things external to me and thus ends in all the catastrophic effects of fortune. *In other words, if you believe in good or bad luck, you are an Aristotelian*. But again, why? Because Aristotle's most crucial category is the category of the possible. For Descartes the belief in fortune necessarily implies that one judges that fortune may be possible.[33] We desire things that are independent from our will because we believe that they are possible to attain. But we judge the way we judge and desire the way we desire only because we do not know "all the causes which contribute to each effect," because we ignore the true nature of causal relations, and because we do not know how these things are determined, so we *hope* for a lucky outcome. Believing in fortune, we disregard what we know (namely that we do not know how things will turn out and that we cannot influence them). Furthermore, by not assuming the knowledge that we have (namely that we know that we do not know certain things and we know we cannot influence them), we act as if we did not know what we know, which is the *origin of hope* (and fear). Hope for good fortune results from such an error of our thought and always produces the belief in a chimera. For if we assumed the knowledge that we have (the knowledge of a lack of knowledge about these things), we would not judge these things to be possible. Rather we would consider them to be "absolutely impossible."[34] We would assume the absolute impossibility of good or bad luck. The fatalist does not believe in luck at all.

From Fortune to Providence

Hope results from a disregard of one's own lack of knowledge and is grounded in acting *as if we did not know that we did not know*. Descartes writes, "We must . . . utterly reject the common opinion that there is a Fortune outside us which causes things to happen or not to happen, just as it pleases. And we must recognize that everything is guided by divine Providence, whose eternal decree is infallible and immutable to such an extent that . . . we must consider everything that affects us to occur of necessity and as it were by fate, so that it would be wrong for us to desire things to happen in any other way."[35] Descartes opposes divine providence to fortune (explicitly siding with Franciscus Gomarus, who defended predestination against Jacobus Arminius).[36] He argues that *a true rationalist needs to be a fatalist* if she wants to avoid believing in and desiring something against her own better knowledge, *if she wants to remain a rationalist* and seeks to assume what she knows. But does the same problem emerge here in another form? To avoid the erroneous judgment that something is possible but depends on good fortune, we need to assume that everything depends on God's predestined plan. However, with this shift we recognize that "except for matters it has determined to be dependent on our free will . . . we must consider their outcome to be wholly fated and immutable," and we must "take care to pick out just what depends only on us, so as to limit our desire to that alone."[37] With the affirmation of divine providence we learn again how to discriminate between what does and what does not depend on us. Yet we learn what depends on us by affirming that *that which depends on us was determined to depend on us by something that does not depend on us*, namely God's providence.

Therefore the affirmation of absolute necessity enables us to make better judgments than any belief in fortune could ever do and does not in any way lead to a suspension of our judgment. Rather "we must not fail to consider the reasons which make [external things] more or less predictable." If there is, for example, "some place to which we might travel by two different routes . . . we should not be indifferent as to which one we choose. . . . Reason insists that we choose the route which is usually the safer." Being a fatalist does not lead to inaction or the abandonment of judgment. What we recognize and accept in cases that are not dependent on our will are our own limitations. This recognition leads to the insight that "whatever evil may befall us . . . was inevitable from our point of view, [and] we had no reason to wish to be exempt from it."[38] Not believing in fortune, abolishing the idea of hope and good luck, and believing in divine providence necessarily imply *assuming the worst*. Providence necessarily implies fatalism.

It follows from this argument that if we do not believe in fortune, we abolish not only all hope but also fear. This is why Descartes can state, "One of the main points in my own ethical code is to love life without fearing death."[39] Only in this way can we develop a proper concept of contingency, through the mediation of the idea of absolute necessity. If something bad happens to me, by believing that God had determined this occurrence since eternity, I simply affirm the necessity of what happened. It thus makes absolutely no sense to feel remorse (or to have feared the bad outcome). In this way I assume that the bad thing happening to me was "inevitable" because I always already assumed its occurrence anyhow when I mapped out what was in my power to do and what was not. Again this does not make me into a stoic. Rather I gain "complete satisfaction" even when something bad happens to me. Why? Simply because when "we had reason only to do the best that our intellect was able to recognize," the evil that happened to us was not possible but predestined to happen and hence absolutely necessary.[40] If I accept that even if I do my best I might nonetheless suffer evil, I cannot blame either fortune or myself. I simply experience what was predestined. I accept the full impact of the necessity of contingency, which indicates the limit of what I could have done. But this can be done only by affirming the idea of absolute necessity, of providence. Only if we do our best and nonetheless expect the worst without fear are we able to direct our desire and will appropriately. Fatalism consists in assuming the worst and not fearing it, as it is not fortune but necessity that brings it about.

Providence entails the notion of the necessity of contingency, because by simply relying on ourselves we cannot know in advance when and how providence will strike. Therefore when providence does intervene, its occurrence *necessarily* strikes us as being *contingent*. But one does not read and interpret this contingent event as being simply contingent because one can escape the idea of fortune only by assuming its necessity. The idea of something contingent happening to me therefore implies that (1) I know what I know (namely that I do not know), that (2) I experience something I did not foresee (because I could not), and that (3) I do not blame it on fortune but assume its complete necessity (due to point 1). This peculiar structure suggests that the evil thing that happens to me does not have a meaning that I could ever understand. If it did, I could just learn through a future occurrence what it meant. This would lead to my accepting fortune, not necessity, as its cause. I assume the necessity of something that happens to me, although from my point of view it appears to be contingent. By doing so I do not commit an error in judgment and fully embrace my knowledge. *What happens to me due to divine providence is ultimately necessarily contingent (as I am not God) and contingently necessary (as God decided what happens to me due to reasons inaccessible and hence meaningless to me). In short, it is important to emphasize both the necessity of contingency as well as the contingency of necessity.*

God the Extimate

If there is divine providence, can one imagine (judging and discriminating properly between what depends on us and what does not) a realm of freedom in which I remain sovereign and untouched by external occurrences that depend on divine providence? Does this distinction of the inside and the outside risk reintroducing a realm of natural capacities (granted by God) and hence another version of Aristotelianism, maybe one similar to Erasmus's? Descartes is quite outspoken in his letters about this problem. Let us take a closer look at two astonishing passages:

> I resign myself to do for my part whatever I regard as my duty and submit myself for the rest to the providence which rules the world. Knowing it is that providence which gave me the small beginnings [of ideas and insights], I hope that the same providence will give me the grace to complete it, if it is useful for its glory, and if not, I wish to give up all desire to do so.[41]

> All the reasons which prove the existence of God, and that he is the first and immutable cause of all the effects which do not depend upon the free will of human beings, likewise prove in the same manner that he is also the cause of all those that depend upon it. For . . . he would not be sovereignly perfect if something could occur in the world that did not

come entirely from him. . . . Philosophy alone suffices for the knowledge that the least thought cannot enter the mind of man if God has not wished and willed from all eternity that it enter therein.[42]

What makes these passages so interesting? First, Descartes clearly indicates to what extent free will, which makes up the substance of thought, depends on divine providence. This is to say that even what is in our power is never truly in our power. It is only in our power if God grants us this power. There is no thought without God's willing this very thought. As Descartes already stated in his *Meditations*, "The more I incline in one direction—either because I understand . . . or because of a divinely produced disposition of my inner thought—the freer is my choice."[43] My thoughts are mine—especially when they are free—only because God has determined them to be what they are. There are no thoughts without God. So my freedom is determined by something that is external to me but occurs within my innermost kernel. God is what determines my inside from the outside, an outside that at the same time is different from the outside of nature. By affirming God's providence, I get rid of the idea that there is anything within me, a natural capacity, for example, that is wholly interior, something that could remain untouched by *God, who is extimate*. This makes "dualism explode from the inside."[44] In order to arrive at a proper understanding of true externality, we also need to get rid of the idea of an already given internality.

Belief in fortune amounts to a weak understanding of externality because it rests on the idea that there is something that I am still able to do. Although it seems to draw a distinction between external and internal causes, such belief ultimately suspends this distinction as it misses the crucial point that a proper externality determines me much more fundamentally than any external object ever could. To understand this point we must reconstruct Descartes's concept of God. Descartes develops it inter alia in his *Discourse on Method*, when he expounds a version of his cogito argument.[45] He starts from a simple fact: I am able to doubt because I know I can err. From this we can infer that we are able to doubt because we have had the experience of failure. We are able to doubt because we know that we are not perfect. This fact makes it possible for us to construe the concept of perfection through negation, because if we understand our failure, we attain the concept of lack and error, the proper understanding of which already implies the existence of its opposite. The experience of something negative negatively implies its own negation. Perfection is the negatively implied negation of the negation we experienced. It is (negatively) contained in the very concept of lack. Lack therefore becomes reflexive and leads to its logical opposite. We thereby gain the idea that there has to be something that lacks lack, that is, something that is perfect. When we experience failure and seek to understand it, we inevitably discover within ourselves the idea of perfection. We are then logically forced to imagine the negation of what we experienced as negation. Because we can err and fail, we have to think of God, since this is how God determines our thoughts. And if our own imperfections result from our constitution, from our being composed of two different substances (body and soul), perfection necessarily has to suspend the source of imperfection.

This reasoning leads Descartes to deduce that something perfect—whose classical name is, of course, "God"—has to exist,[46] since that which is perfect would not be perfect if it did not exist. Along these lines he writes, "Many are convinced that there is some difficulty in knowing God, and in even knowing what their soul is. The reason for this is that they never raise their mind above things which can be perceived by the senses:

they are so used to thinking of things only by imagining them (a way of thinking especially suited to material things) that whatever is unimaginable seems to them unintelligible."[47] This difficulty emerges from the understanding that one cannot simply imagine or picture God. If God cannot have a body, then we have to imagine God differently. Anything that has a body appears in a world and in a discourse, which means that God has to be nondiscursive and unworldly, even if we must try to grasp him from within a discourse and from within a world to which he has to be logically "prior" since he created it. He is the postdiscursively graspable prediscursive, the lack of lack. He is what we cannot comprehend discursively (by imagining him).

But we can know that there is something that we cannot comprehend. In other words, we can comprehend that there is something that we cannot comprehend: "It is possible to know that God is infinite and all powerful although our soul being finite, cannot grasp or conceive it. In the same way we can touch a mountain with our hands but we cannot put our arms around it as we could put them around a tree."[48] We can think "God," but we think him as that which we cannot think. Hence we have a clear and distinct idea of the unthinkable that is completely rational. We are forced to think the unthinkable as that which we cannot think. There is a "clarity of the incomprehensible. . . . There is a clear and distinct incomprehensibility of God which does not lead up to be a confused notion."[49] The act of thinking God is one case when one is able to think the unthinkable. It is not only possible to do so but in fact necessary. As soon as one commits an error in judgment and seeks to understand it, one is forced to think not only the concept of error but also the concept of God and thus the very origin of thought. To put it differently, as soon as we reach the "I think," we are forced to think what we can think of only as that which we cannot think. "At the center of the Cogito" there is thus something "not immanent, but rather transcendent."[50] God is immanent to our thought as we cannot think without thinking him, but he transcends our capacities. He is what we can think only as that which we cannot think. We are therefore forced to think something that exceeds the capacity of thought.

What do we think when we think that which exceeds its own being-thought? We think the necessity of contingency as well as the contingency of necessity. What is thought here is that which creates all truths and hence determines the truth of thought itself.[51] This truth is necessarily linked to the necessity of contingency because God's will is so free that nothing he wills or does is necessary. This is why it can be characterized by the concept of the infinite, of "actual infinity" and not of Aristotelian potential infinity.[52] Sartre demonstrated that from our perspective God's freedom must be identical to absolute contingency.[53] God creates as he likes, freely and indifferently. Being forced to think what we cannot think leads us to confront the necessity of sheer contingency. But if necessary contingency stands at the foundation of God's providence and everything he created, then, in thinking it, we also attain a fundamental characteristic of truth. This is what makes Descartes unique: there are eternal truths, yet they have not existed forever. Rather God has created them, and thus their creation was necessarily contingent. We think truths are necessarily contingent if we are forced to think that which we cannot think. In this sense Descartes's God is so free that he does not care about logical constraints or consistency, as he is the one who created logics.[54] For God's "power is beyond our grasp. In general we can assert that God can do everything that is within our grasp but not that he cannot do what is beyond our grasp. It would be rash to think that our imagination reaches as far as his power."[55] In confronting the unthinkable within our thought, we encounter something so contingent that it suspends all laws, something that is, strictly and logically speaking, constitutively illegal and radically heteronomous. Within me I find an Other that is so Other that I can never integrate it or include it in my inner realm of thought. In other words, as soon as I reach the innermost realm of thought, the cogito, I am thrown out of myself in a more radical manner than I can think or imagine. Therefore an immanent cause forces me to think that there is something within me that fully escapes me.

But as it is this heteronomous Other that is the unthinkable ground from which truths emerge, they emerge from a necessarily contingent act of creation. In this sense truths and laws are not compatible (not even the laws of thought), which is why the advent of thought, that is, its creation by God, can be thought only as that which cannot be thought, for the creation of truths can violate even the laws of logic.[56] Descartes's point can be made even more precise: It is not that thinking God only means obtaining insight into the necessity of contingency, but rather that in the concept of "God" necessity and contingency become indistinguishable. If God wills something, he wills it as necessary and for eternity, which is why and how he creates eternal truths. At the same time, his will is conceivable only as not being bound to any laws and therefore as being utterly contingent. It follows that in God necessity and contingency become undecidable and indistinguishable, as whatever he contingently wills becomes necessary due to fully contingent reasons. His "actions were completely free, yet were also completely necessary."[57] Another version of this argument states that if God can be thought only as that which cannot be thought, and true thinking for Descartes always means clearly distinguishing one thing from another, then thinking of God must mean thinking of him as completely different from all differences, as that which can clearly and distinctly be thought of as exceeding our distinguishing power, as that which is indistinguishable and therefore unique. This is because, as one can argue with Henri Gouhier, "the idea of God . . . is clear and distinct as it represents a reality beyond any clear and distinct representation."[58] This construct also holds for the distinction between necessity and contingency. The three consequences of the idea of divine providence become clarified: first, the notion implies a rigid belief in contingency that exceeds any kind of weak contingency of fortune; second, it implies that we must treat that which happens to us contingently, given the absolute necessity of God's will; and third, the notion is linked to the peculiar insight that one has to accept that one will never be able to know how God predestined all things since one can think of him only as that which one cannot think, as something that is constitutively undecidable for us. "God," this "new idea of God,"[59] names in Descartes a unique undecidability, which is the contingent ground of all eternal and necessary truths. Thus being a fatalist is the precondition for truly thinking of God as that which is undecidably necessary and contingent. For Descartes only a fatalist can truly think contingency.

But if we are forced to think of God as that which we cannot think, we are thinking him in four subsequent steps: (1) we think the lack of lack; (2) we think the being of the lack of lack; (3) we characterize this being of the lack of lack as infinite; and (4) thereby infinity becomes the infinity of his will and is identified with the undecidability between necessity and contingency. Yet if infinity is a characteristic of God's will, then a wonderfully paradoxical and surprising consequence results: Descartes argues that "God's will does not seem any greater than mine when considered as will in the essential and strict sense." Thinking that which one can think only as unthinkable (thinking of God through the infinity of his free will) leads to the consequence that I am thereby forced to think freedom. Not only God's, but also my own. I am forced to do what I cannot do, think what I cannot think, and it is precisely in that moment that I arrive at the very concept of freedom. Freedom is thus at first defined as being forced to do what one cannot do because it is not in one's capacity. Yet precisely by doing something that one cannot do, one is forced to encounter freedom, one's "likeness of God."[60] Freedom therefore can be thought only as that which one cannot think. As soon as I ascribe or predicate it to myself, I lose my freedom. This, we could argue, is "a new, different logic" of freedom.[61]

The Freedom of a Fatalist

Fatalism turns out to be a precondition not only for thinking contingency proper and for avoiding attachment to natural causations, fortune, for getting rid of hope and fear, but also for freedom. What does this mean for the notion of freedom? If the essence of human beings at least partially consists of the freedom of the will, and if this very freedom can be thought by thinking God as that which I cannot think, in that case my own essence is beyond my grasp. For the same reason this essence is no longer a substantial essence, since I can think it only as that which I cannot think. But it is also not nothing(ness). Although Sartre argues otherwise, Descartes is *not* a Sartrean.[62] My essence is neither a given essence nor its negation, as both of these options can quite easily be thought. Rather, if I am most God-like in my essence, then this essence must be neither something nor nothing. It must be something that is more than something and less than nothing. If God is the creator of nature, then my essence can neither be simply natural nor simply nonnatural, that is, cultural, for, again, both can quite easily be thought. Only one option is possible: my essence is unnatural. But at the same time, as *The Passions of the Soul* demonstrates, I am not simply my free will but also a body, and I appear in this world as a natural being with a body. My freedom is unnatural, and at the same time I am a natural being. Thus one must infer that there *is* in some sense no relation between body and soul, between the two different substances of which I am composed. Yet there *is* an embodiment of this nonrelation or, in short, there is an unrelation. This ultimately means the following: The human being is the embodiment of the unrelation between nature (which is determined by external causality) and unnature (freedom). It is important that here the *un-* appears twice in this formula, since this reduplication indicates the difference between a Cartesian and a Spinozist position. For the latter, to cut a very long story short, ultimately the human being is a relational embodiment that is related to something unnatural at its core (God), whereas the former emphasizes the constitutive embodiment of an unrelation between the two and only thereby avoids substantializing (or naturalizing) it.

This is also the background against which we can see why we have to oppose all forms of naturalizing our essence. And as naturalization—which has always been one of the most crucial operations of any kind of reactionary ideology—follows from the universalization of natural causality that underlies any Aristotelianism, we absolutely have to oppose any form of Aristotelianism. My essence, which is freedom, cannot be natural and naturalized because this naturalization would introduce a relation between my body and my soul. I would then be an embodiment of related substances, which is precisely what needs to be avoided. In short, my freedom can never be a capacity. And what is Aristotelianism if not a gigantic and intricate effort to expound on the concept of capacity? For if we think that freedom is completely in our power, a capacity at hand that depends on fortune when we seek to actualize it, then we encounter a few difficulties "in deciding upon the means of putting [this freedom] into effect." This "gives rise to irresolution" that can be overcome solely by "courage or boldness."[63]

Descartes also calls this courage "generosity." It is the courage that consists in "the power of regeneration or rebirth," which makes us "discover that we bear the image and resemblance of God."[64] Only a courageous embrace of fatalism can help us overcome Aristotle. Fatalism thereby becomes a fundamental requirement of any Cartesian rationalist position. It counters a false understanding of freedom that identifies freedom with a capacity, which relies on fortune and hence natural causality. And it affirms that if freedom is not a capacity, it must be something else: a result. It results from something contingent happening to me, from something so contingent that it is conceptually unthinkable. There needs to be something that makes freedom possible. I am free only when I am contingently forced to be. This is what it means to be forced to move from thinking the cogito to thinking what I can think only as unthinkable, namely God. This in turn compels me to think of freedom as something beyond a simple thought that I have. Rather this very shift that makes me think freedom as that which I cannot think forces me to be free. It not only liberates me from Aristotelianism but also forces me to think what I cannot think. And this means that the very form of this thought *is* freedom. Freedom is thereby not the content of my thought but its form.

That thinking is forced to think what it cannot think means that the very notion of thinking implies that its proper concept originates from a determination that does not originate in thought itself but from somewhere else. The same also holds for freedom. I am forced to think, and I am forced to be free. Such is the freedom of a fatalist that emerges out of what forces me to think what I cannot think (other than as what I cannot think). I am unfree as soon as I conceive of my freedom as something that is in my power. Freedom turns into a capacity. Only by acting and thinking as if I were not free—that is, being a fatalist—do I affirm a determination that I cannot deduce from my capacities, namely that I am free only when something happens to me that forces me to be free and forces me to make a choice. Thereby I do not simply become the instrument of the big Other, of God's will. Rather I become even more responsible for my deeds because everything is determined, but it is entirely unclear how. This is why, in some sense, I should not care about how things are determined, since even the Other (God) is also determined by contingency, which is to say that God has no plan about his plan either. (He is also determined by contingency.) For Descartes, I have to assume that I am determined (I am forced to be free or to think by something that does not spring from my thought or freedom), and this implies that in the heart of the human being, at the origin of true human actions, lies something determining the human in a manner that cannot leave us indifferent. Through fatalism one affirms the impossible possibility that true freedom is possible, although there is no objective guarantee (neither in me nor in the world) for it. Simply put, *only a fatalist can be free*. This is because there is nothing to hope for, there is nothing to rely on, and there is nothing in our power. But this helps us avoid falling for the trap of acting as if we were free. What we can thus derive from Descartes is a second principle of a contemporary provisional morality: *Act as if you were not free!*

3

From Kant to Schmid (and Back)

The End of All Things

Submit yourself to the rule of a necessity from which you cannot escape.
—Denis Diderot, *Jacques the Fatalist*

Critique of Practical Reason . . . *I must mention here* en passant
*that the concept of "the practical" should not be confused with
the degenerate concept that has become current nowadays.*
—Theodor W. Adorno, *Problems of Moral Philosophy*

But it is of greatest importance to be content with providence.
—Immanuel Kant, "Conjectural Beginning of Human History"

A "Groundwork" of Fatalism

In the historical move from religious to philosophical fatalism, from defending predestination against the assumption
of free will to defending it in order to undo the Aristotelian
identification of freedom and capacity, fatalism appears at the
center of any properly rationalist position. It can therefore seem
predestined that in the late eighteenth century the claim arises
that rational beings—simply because they are *rational* beings—
cannot but be fatalists. Peculiarly this claim was presented as
the consequence of a position that seems to argue for the opposite, namely for linking rationality and an absolute capacity of
freedom. How did this happen? In 1785 Kant's *Groundwork of*

the Metaphysics of Morals was taken by some of its readers as a demonstration of the necessity of practical fatalism, even if the author had not intended this. This interpretation of the *Groundwork* then provided the basis for reading the entirety of Kant's philosophy as a complex plea for a rationalist fatalism. Before turning to one of the most impressive of Kant's interpreters, it is instructive to first clarify how this interpretation was possible at all. How and why can one read Kant as providing the metaphysical foundations for practical fatalism?

The *Groundwork* has a peculiar structure. Its three sections all deal with transitions: first, the transition from common rational to philosophical moral cognition; second, from popular moral philosophy to the metaphysics of morals; third, from the metaphysics of morals to pure practical reason. It is clear that we are confronted here not only with a transition into metaphysics but also with a metaphysics that is essentially concerned with transitions (from everyday life to pure reason and back to a different practice of everyday life). The idea behind this structure seems to arise from the introduction of a distinction between commonsense thought and philosophical thought. This distinction is generative of the concept of morality—the latter emerges from a critique, and it is the other side of common sense. Morality must be distinct from the way one commonly perceives the world because otherwise morality would depend on the commonality of perception. But common sense is not only contingent but also rarely even exists as a collectively binding phenomenon. Morality grounded on common sense would thus be quite shaky, and a shaky ground for moral judgments and actions is practically no ground at all. Also, if morality could be derived from common experience, then it could be explained by experiential, that is, natural causality. If this were the case there would simply no longer be any morality: natural entities and phenomena are not free.

One would thus end up with a sort of bad determinism, a bad fatalism that abolishes freedom.

Kant clearly does not go in this direction. A quick glance at the titles of the *Groundwork*'s sections makes clear that the distinction between commonsense approaches and a moral philosophy alone is insufficient for grounding morality proper. The book's structure suggests that the temptation for giving a commonsense account of morality resurges within philosophy in the guise of popular moral philosophy. This resurgence results in a struggle between the commonsense conception of morality and a properly metaphysical account of morals.[1] This struggle presents an instructive entry point into Kant's line of argument. If transitions determine the form of the problem, there is no better place to start than the transition from one transition to the next. This is also where the transition from moral philosophy to the metaphysics of morals takes place, which provides the groundwork for critical fatalism.

Kant starts the second section of his book by taking up a simple fact: "It is absolutely impossible by means of experience to make out with complete certainty a single case in which the maxim of an action otherwise in conformity with duty rested simply on moral ground and on representation of one's duty." The problem is that one can find "no certain example" of a truly moral action. Even worse, if we examine empirically a supposedly moral act that took place in the course of history, we will always find the "dear self" lurking behind what first appeared to be noble moral motives. This is to say that examples from our experience can be "*in conformity with* what *duty* commands," but they never seem to be "done *from duty*." People act this way to avoid the consequences of violating their duties, but not for the sake of duty itself. This objection, that any action ultimately appears to rely on self-seeking motives, usually arises when someone demands a concrete example of a true moral deed. For Kant, fulfilling this demand is impossible. There is no experiential paradigm for morality, and this lack produces a fundamental uncertainty. If one begins with empirical examples, it is uncertain whether morality exists at all, "whether any true virtue is to be found in the world."[2] There is no path from experience to morality, and it seems impossible even to phenomenally demonstrate that morality exists.

So what can we do with this dilemma? Kant performs a truly Cartesian maneuver: either only uncertainty is certain and there is no morality (and thus no uncertainty), just the pure laws of nature without freedom; or morality must be grounded differently, namely "prior to all experience, in the idea of a reason determining the will by means of a priori grounds." The impossibility of deriving morality from phenomena means that either morality does not exist or the foundations of morality have to be thought differently. If morality vanishes, that which grounds morality for Kant (freedom) vanishes too, leaving us with nothing but natural causality and total determinism. But because for Kant there is no reason without freedom, reason would disappear along with morality and freedom. This is why a rational being must opt for the second choice. Although it seems impossible to defend morality, it is necessary to do so. Morality must be an a priori ground for all "rational beings."[3] Only in this way does one avoid the destructive consequences of commonsense reasoning.

But how can we do this? Again, in a Cartesian manner, Kant argues that one needs to subtract everything that may present a ground for uncertainty. One needs "a completely isolated metaphysics of morals," subtracted from any kind of anthropology. Taking the human species as the only real subject of morality would make morality human, but it would not inherently link it to reason. If only humans could act morally, what could we say about God? How about other rational beings (say, angels)? We would therefore separate reason and morality and ultimately ground morality in a contingent empirical condition, namely the human one. This is precisely what needs to be avoided, as its consequence would be the abolition of morality tout court. Therefore one needs to isolate the metaphysics of morals from the *anthropos* and its logic. One must also subtract it from theology, since to start from subjective beliefs or divine decrees would again not link morality to the general constitution of rationality but either ground it in unstable, contingent particular estimations or in some kind of external coercion. Morality would thus lose its universal scope and would again not be necessary. It would also follow that morality could not be conceived of as immanent to the constitution of a rational being but would ultimately have external origins, thus separating it from the concept of freedom. One also needs to subtract any kind of physics from the grounding of morality, since physical theories and explanations focus solely on the laws of phenomena and their relations. Because of this subtractive maneuver, "we see philosophy put in fact in a precarious position, which is to be firm even though there is nothing in heaven or on earth from which it depends or on which it is based."[4] What is this nothing on which morality is based? Where is it located?

Subtracting theology, anthropology, and physics allows Kant to come to "the universal concept of a rational being as such." The nothing upon which morality is based thus finds its place in the heart of the rational being. This is where Kant begins his properly critical endeavor. As this being, just like any other, has a specific constitution (a nature), and because "everything in nature works in accordance with laws," one can analyze the laws that are constitutive for the rational being as such. Here Kant specifies that in contrast to other natural entities, "only a rational being has the capacity to act in accordance with the representation of laws, that is, in accordance with principles, or has a will. Since reason is required for the derivation of actions from laws, the will is nothing other than practical reason." Because of its rationality, a rational being does not simply follow laws mechanically but is able to deduce its actions from laws. Hence it must have a will. The concept of the will names the capacity of a rational being to determine itself such that it acts as a rational being (inferring actions from laws). This means that the will is another name for practical reason. Here we can see that there are two options concerning the relation between reason and will. The first is that "reason infallibly determines the will." Thus the actions following from it are completely determined by reason. The will wills only what reason demands and is "completely in conformity" with it.[5] This means the will is determined in such a way that what is objectively necessary (what reason commands to do) is also subjectively necessary (what the will wills). But the second option is that reason does not fully determine the will, and thus the will is also determined by other sources, say, inclinations or interests, which may not conform to reason. Such actions that are only partially determined by reason would then entail an element of contingency at their basis. So the two options account for a will that acts in a fully rational manner and for a will that acts in an only partially rational manner. The will therefore may or may not (completely) will what reason commands.

This distinction grounds, but is at the same time grounded in, the difference between two kinds of commands of reason: hypothetical and categorical. Hypothetical imperatives, as Kant calls the first kind, command actions as necessary means for attaining an end. An action is thus evaluated as being good for the sake of attaining something else. In contrast, a categorical imperative represents "an action as objectively necessary of itself" and "as in itself good." The hypothetical imperative judges merely the possible or actual purpose of an action, whereas the categorical

imperative judges "the action to be of itself objectively necessary without reference to some purpose, that is, even apart from
any other end." The categorical imperative considers neither
the content of the action nor its consequences but only "the
form and the principle from which the action itself follows . . .
let the result be what it may." Similar to Descartes, Kant can
argue that by following categorical imperatives one will never
have to repent or revoke anything. Here one is faced with the
intricacy of Kant's argument. Acting in complete conformity
with reason—not only acting as a rational being but also willing
in an absolutely moral way, subtracted from all contingencies
and particularities of the phenomenal world—means to stick
to a form and principle no matter what may result from it. All
hypothetical imperatives contain some remnant of experiential
relation: the phenomenal world abides. Thus they cannot ground
morality proper. Only pure reason can do so in the form of the
categorical imperative, which therefore "alone has the tenor
of a practical law. . . . The unconditional command leaves the
will no discretion with respect to the opposite [*dem Willen kein
Belieben . . . frei läßt* literally means 'leaving the will no arbitrary
choice'], so that it alone brings with it that necessity which we
require of a law." The categorical imperative is the form in which
pure reason determines the will in such a way that the will has
no choice but to follow what reason commands. It thereby wills
according to a maxim—that is, a "subjective principle"—that
conforms to what reason judges to be objectively necessary.
Practical law and maxim of the will (what and how it is willed),
objective necessity and subjective necessity, coincide. They
become indistinguishable. This indistinguishability is not based
on a free decision but, paradoxical as it may seem, on an *a priori
product*, which is why, according to the terminology of the *Critique of Pure Reason*, the categorical imperative is "an a priori
synthetic-practical proposition."[6] In the *Critique of Pure Reason*,

Kant famously distinguished between analytic and synthetic judgments, a distinction that is instructive to recall in this context. Analytic judgments are clarifications and articulate and make explicit what is already contained in a concept, whereas synthetic judgments extend and expand the scope of a concept by "adding [*hinzufügen*]" a connection between the concept and another one. Therefore in the case of synthetic judgments the question is how to add and bring about a connection, a "really new acquisition [*Erwerb* (B) / *Anbau* (A)]" in an a priori manner. This is why Kant investigated the possibility of synthetic judgments a priori.[7] In the present context the question is: how to conceive of a priori synthetic-practical propositions?

The Third Cognition and the Double-Count

Kant answers this question in the following way: "I connect the deed with the will, without a presupposed condition from any inclination, a priori and hence necessarily (though only objectively, i.e., under the idea of a reason having complete control over all subjective motives)." The will is unconditionally connected with an action when the principle that guides it in its practice (the willing of the will) has such a form as if it were not subjective but objective, as if it were not a particular principle but a universal one. This is why Kant can formulate this proposition in various ways, all of which make the same point. To mention just a few: "*act as if the maxim of your action were to become by your will a* universal law of nature"; "*act in accordance with a maxim that can at the same time make itself a universal law*"; "act on a maxim that at the same time contains in itself its own universal validity for every rational being"; and "I ought to act in such or such a way even though I have not willed anything else."[8]

These formulations supposedly express the same logical structure while emphasizing different aspects of it. Kant derives from them the concepts of duty, of an end in itself, and of autonomy. In order to make the link between Kant and fatalism more explicit, the last of Kant's formulations proves interesting. We must, however, insist that the ambiguities of Kant's original formulation are lost in the English translation. He writes, "Ich soll so handeln, ob ich gleich nichts anderes wollte," which one can read in at least three different ways. First, one may translate this as "I ought to act in such a way, even though I have not willed anything else." In other words, I act in such a way that I am in conformity with the moral law, although I didn't will anything else. "Ob ich gleich nichts anderes wollte," then, is rendered as "although I have not willed" except that which I ought to will. "Ob . . . gleich" is given the meaning "although." Second, one may render Kant's formulation as "even though I have willed nothing else," which implies, as Rado Riha has convincingly demonstrated, that there is "no preconditioned matter, no object and no end that is sought to be attained through the willing actions—*and nonetheless one wills.* The categorical imperative is thus not at all only characterized by the fact that by means of it the mere willing is determined by putting aside all matter of the will. Rather by means of it the will is brought to continue willing, although the will wills nothing anymore: it is Nothing itself . . . as 'objectless object' that should be willed here."[9] The will thus wills nothing, the "nothing in heaven or on earth from which it depends."[10] This interpretation implies willing the "absence of the object as object."[11] The will is thereby directed to its own pure form, which is the definition of freedom. But this is a freedom that paradoxically can be said to ground the moral law, that is, the categorical imperative. Third, we may read Kant's formulation such that one takes "ob ich gleich" to mean "as if." In this case we would translate it as "I ought to act as if I have not willed anything else."

The first reading emphasizes that my will coincides with what I ought to do anyway regardless of its content. The second stresses that I can act in conformity with what I ought to do only when I completely subtract everything from my will and nonetheless continue to will. And the third interpretation stresses that I ought to act in such a way that I will as if I willed what I ought to do. One should emphasize that these three accentuations all belong together: Only if I act as if I willed precisely what the law of reason commands me to do can I properly claim to will freely, and I only really will freely when I will in such a way that my will directly coincides with the moral law. Yet this can be done only if I do not will any concrete matter or object but rather the absent ground of the will itself. I can will freely only if I act as if I willed only what I ought to will, and what I ought to will is nothing objective but rather the very coincidence of the will and the law. Consequently, if these conditions do not apply, although I might seem to will freely, I do not properly will but am rather determined. If I do not will what I ought to will, I am not only determined and thus not free but I am also not willing anymore (since to will implies freedom): *either I am forced to will what I ought to will or I am determined otherwise.* It is this structure that provides the very ground for the emergence of fatalism, since I will only if I will nothing, which is to say that I will only if my maxim and the law coincide. This in turn can occur only if I act as if I willed only what the law commands. Otherwise there is no (free) will. *Either I obey* (the moral law) *or I obey* (natural determinations). With this emphasis there does not seem to be any choice involved—although Kant himself does not explicitly draw this conclusion.

Here it is important to highlight the consequences that Kant himself draws from the various formulations of the categorical imperative. This comprises the very move from the metaphysics of morals to the critique of pure practical reason. What is at stake here is a more precise definition of the will: the will is "a kind of causality of living beings insofar as they are rational," and it therefore must be free and independent from heteronomous determinations. This concept of freedom, however, is only "negative and therefore unfruitful for insight into its essence." But because Kant has shown that there is a positive concept of freedom, namely that "a free will and a will under moral laws are one and the same," it is precisely the form of the moral law that defines the concept of freedom as a positive characteristic of the will. Here Kant states that if we take into account the fact that the positive concept of freedom is a synthetic proposition, and "synthetic propositions are possible only in this way: that the two cognitions are bound together by their connection with a third in which they are both to be found," the question arises "what this third cognition is."[12]

Kant's answer is dialectically intriguing: it is the very distinction between the noumenal and the phenomenal realm. The distinction between these two spheres is what grounded the pure metaphysics of morals in the beginning. At the same time, this very distinction is constitutive of any living rational being. A rational being belongs to the phenomenal world (it is embodied), yet it also belongs to the noumenal realm (it is a free will). As a result the rational being is a manifestation of this very distinction. If the two spheres are truly separate, the living rational being is an embodiment of what is distinct, of what is nonrelated, that is, of a nonrelation (recall Descartes). The living rational being must count itself as belonging to the phenomenal world (because it lives) and to the noumenal, "to the *intellectual* world, of which however [it] has no further cognition" (because it is rational).[13] Yet because it must count itself twice, a blind spot arises: the very impossibility of relating the two counts. There is no count of the two counts, or, put differently, there is no common measure. Because of this lack of measure, there is "an embodiment of the blind spot that sustains the difference between phenomena and noumena."[14] This new space is comparable to what Nicole Loraux calls a "bond of division," which presents a third space in which the two separate spheres can be found.[15] The double-count thus entails that the living rational being is part of the noumenal and the phenomenal spheres, yet the noumenal sphere is what can be thought only when all phenomenal determinations are subtracted. If phenomenality is fully determined by laws of nature, and if the noumenal is also lawfully governed, real freedom resides in the very form of the distinction between the two realms, which at the same time indispensably relates two determinisms to one another. Of this peculiarity Kant says that one can only "comprehend its *incomprehensibility*."[16] Yet if this double-count enables a distinction between natural determinism on the one hand and another form of causality on the other, do we thereby escape determinism?

Moral Revolution

This question was first raised by a truly committed Kantian, Carl Christian Erhard Schmid (1761–1812), who is completely forgotten today. To my knowledge none of his works has been translated into English. He was one of *the* main authorities on Kantian philosophy in his time. He taught Kant to Novalis and gave an intricate answer to the question raised above. His answer was that one does not overcome determinism in the realm of noumenal freedom. Rather, precisely because of the nature of freedom, one ends up with another kind of determinism. In this context Schmid coined the notion "intelligible fatalism." The expression appears for the first time in his *Essay on Moral Philosophy*, published in 1790. Its second edition appeared two years later, and the changes and supplements Schmid added nearly doubled its length. This work claims to be fully faithful to Kant and presents a Kantian critical fatalism.

Schmid seeks to expound moral philosophy's "primary fundamental doctrines." The starting points for this venture are the "dark or clear concepts of duty, right and wrong, virtue and vice, good and evil," which "the common sense of any human being entails and discovers within itself from its first development on."[17] These concepts cannot be denied, and human beings cannot fail to respect them, even if they sometimes are tempted to. Because of the universality of these concepts, the "philosophy of morality is the noblest and most interesting part of the whole of philosophy," and it has a direct effect on the "everyday life" of everyone.[18] Everyday life is directly influenced by a moral philosophical investigation not only because of the universalist scope of its concepts but also due to the imminently practical nature of these concepts. All practical concepts are related to the determination of the will or its actions, and the objects of practical philosophy are therefore the "ideas of possible affections and actions determined to produce practical rules, that is, general judgments about what . . . one ought to do." Such ideas are ends that can either be contingent, partially necessary, or unconditionally necessary. Practical philosophy thus entails an investigation of the arts that deal with contingent ends (medicine), partially necessary ends (doctrines of sagacity), and unconditional ends (morality). The last defines the business of moral philosophy, which deals with determining the "final end or the fate of man." Schmid thereby has precisely defined the scope of what will be treated within his moral philosophy, and this treatment will affect the fate of everyone. If moral philosophy fulfills its task, it will "bring about an imminent revolution" affecting all spheres of life.[19]

How to Do Things with Actions: The Moral World

In order to achieve this goal, Schmid's moral philosophy seeks to unfold "unchangeable and universally valid principles" that can only "lie in the essence of reason itself." This universalism implies opposing any form of moral skepticism, empiricism, mysticism, and moral sensualism. The universalist dimension and its revolutionary character can be upheld only from the position of a moral rationalism, which is defined by constructing a *negative diagonal* to these other positions. It is defined, first, by the antiskeptical claim that there are universally valid principles; second, by the antimystical claim that these principles are not external to reason; third, by the antiempiricist and antisensualist claim that neither phenomena nor our senses entail these principles; fourth, by the properly rationalist claim that they are originally contained in pure reason; and fifth, by the claim that they are applied by reason to the form of the sensuously given material. Moral philosophy for Schmid hence investigates what is absolutely necessary: "absolutely necessary practical rules," the "absolutely necessary end," the "absolutely necessary driving force [*Triebfeder*]," and the "absolutely necessary condition by means of which the will is able to follow the moral law." Those principles, as in Kant, must be what I pursue, "not because I will something else, but because I am a rational being."[20] Therefore the subject of inquiry is the form and not some concrete matter of the will.[21] As in Kant, there is no precondition, no presumed material in the concept of morality at stake here. There are only "practical laws." These laws define the difference between what is a good and what is an evil deed, and this distinction must be necessary. Here Schmid also distinguishes moral philosophy from moral theology, since if morality were to rely on God's will, God's will would have to be knowable for us. Otherwise it would not have apodictic necessity but rather hinge on contingency. Even worse, it would imply "a coercion that would rob my virtue of its entire inner value."[22] Moral philosophy in Schmid therefore, as in Kant, proves the necessity of morality without theology.

Schmid then excludes a series of concepts that cannot provide a stable ground for morality. First, he excludes the concept of moral perfection that was defended by Christian Wolff or the Stoics, since it can involve a moment of inner pleasure (and is hence not a universal but a particular end). Next, he excludes the concept of moral sentiments or affects, as defended by Adam Smith, Helvetius, Locke, and others, which ultimately proves to be obscure and indeterminate and thus not absolute and necessary. Finally, he excludes the concept of happiness that involves the notions of well-being, beatitude, and bliss as crucial for any eudemonistic ethic. Eudemonism implies physical necessity, a natural law, and not a moral one, and therefore leads to the problematic consequence that all physical necessities are presented as morally good.[23] But "if everything is supposed to be good, including physical events and thus that which simply must happen, everything is good in the same way and is thus indifferent." A proper moral philosopher, in Schmid's view, must "clear away all material and empirical rules from the domain of ethics," since they are all based on "*heteronomy*, external legislation," and on human *nature* (even if modified by reason). Just like Kant, Schmid does not derive morality from anthropology, excluding it along with any Aristotelianism, which founds morality on the specific ends of the human form of life. Morality is literally an inhuman concept. The moral rationalist must emphasize and maintain, against heteronomous determinations of morality, that reason is "the highest ethical principle."[24]

Schmid begins with what he calls an "indeterminate formula": "Act rationally, i.e., derive your actions, as regards their content as well as their motivation, from principles of reason; let them be determined by laws of reason."[25] Reason must be the determining instance. Even if human beings do not act rationally, "this has no modifying influence on the principles of reason," whereas empirical conditions can be modified by reason.[26] What does it mean to act rationally? If reason has its own way of producing objects, namely by means of cognition, then rational action means "to make real (to actualize) objects of this cognition."[27] One is able to do so because of the capacity of practical reason. But as there are certain representations in reason that are only partially produced by reason and some that are completely produced by reason, the imperative enjoins us to act in a purely rational manner.

Pure rational representation is "a priori," "of and from principles," "self-acting," "systematic," and "absolutely necessary and universal for all rational beings." To put it differently, purely rational actions are derived from principles, that is, from the most universal rules; they hinge on a priori representations, that is, aim at objects that cannot be derived from experience; and they are autonomous and systematic, that is, rigorous and consistent. Furthermore Schmid classifies them as "absolutely necessary" (because we cannot act differently) and as absolutely universal and free from all sensuous perceptions, material, or sentiment. These aspects emphasize in different ways what it means to act rationally. Thus, for reason, acting rationally is "the *law of nature*." But even if this is the objective structure of rational actions, we can will such an action only if we represent it in the form of an imperative. (Act rationally!) It is here that a crucial question emerges: If man is a rational as well as a sensuous being, then how can we conceive of the relation or nonrelation between man's sensuous being and rational being in such a way that it has relevance for the practice of living rational beings? Schmid answers this question by distinguishing between different forms of actions. First, *sensuous and animal ways of acting* are the mode in which beings endowed solely with sensuous capacities desire to act. None of their actions results from "rules or maxims, which [they] represent to [themselves], but from those which have been unconsciously determined by nature in the constitution of [their] instincts." As the human being is also an animal, if man acts according to his natural instincts, then man acts like an animal. Distinct from this mode are *actions determined by the understanding* (according to represented particular rules with limited validity that may be contingently assembled and are thus only partially necessary), *empirically rational actions* (determined by reason operating under the predominance of a given sensuous and thus contingent material), and *pure rational ways of acting of a sensuous being*. Only the last are in conformity with reason's own laws of nature. From this Schmid derives his first determinate representation of the categorical imperative: "Act in such a way that you could will that your maxim . . . ought to be a universal law for you as well as for all other rational beings."[28]

He continues to purify things more and more to explain how such an imperative is thinkable at all. Beginning with the question of why anyone should obey such an imperative, Schmid argues that we should do so simply because such action is rational, and we cannot question its rationality unless we seek to deny our own rationality. Why we can act this way is "unexplainable," as we can ascertain the existence of our capacities "through their effects (moral laws, commands, judgments, sentiments), not through their own super-sensuous reasons." We can derive the fact that there are human capacities from the effects they have. (Hence the latter strangely precede the former logically.) But what does all this tell us about what is supposed to be a universal end and an unconditional good? It can be only the "free efficacy of a rational will or morality as such," that is to say: an absolute end can be only a pure law that is necessarily unconditional, thus good without exception, internally infinite, and actively realized but also already "actual in its possibility." Even its possibility is already a reality and actuality that differs from what one commonly perceives as reality and actuality: "Reason does not come and go[;] its peculiar good is hence not produced but only revealed in the world of sense." What could be an absolute incentive or motivation? It must be a nonpathological interest. As every pathological interest is interested *in* something, a nonpathological interest is *essentially* interesting. It interests everyone, yet its object is subtracted. Its object cannot be "an object of either hope or fear" but only the moral law. One respects the moral law and oneself as its subject (and as being subjected to it). Respect is the affective expression of a nonpathological interest in the moral law, which is *thereby* actual in its possibility, and it expresses the peculiar relation in which reason, within a rational sensuous being, stands to its sensuous embodiment. Respect is a sentiment of nonrelation, since "the emotion is cognizable, and yet, its ground is only thinkable; its genesis is therefore as incomprehensible as any free action in general."[29]

Based on these arguments, Schmid concludes that one is "compelled by reason" to think "something in itself as the ground layer of that which appears" in an action.[30] This attitude opens up a different perspective on the world. It implies that the highest good can in fact be realized in this world. So we should relate to the world as the space of taking place, as the "splace" of moral action.[31] By redetermining my relation to the world through what is absolutely rationally necessary for me, the world is immediately transformed, revolutionized. A shift of perspective transforms the world from a natural to a moral world. This is where the idea of responsibility emerges: the world will be a moral place "if I will it, i.e., there is no subjective, inner or outer physical obstacle that would be unsurpassable for my serious moral effort."[32] Hence we should not be optimists but engage with the world and will what we ought to will.

But how do we do that? We would need to determine the

structure of that which we cannot comprehend but nonetheless consider to be rationally necessary. In good Kantian manner, Schmid claims that "theoretically, the infinite nature of our limited sensuous capacity of representation makes it *impossible* for us to imagine the existence of such a constitution of the world," yet "practically . . . I am conscious of its unconditional necessity." Acting purely rationally, that is, acting morally, is at the same time impossible and necessary, yet I am forced to do so. Therefore "I will and thus believe" that I can act in this way. Schmid thereby sets up the concept of a commitment that is necessitated by reason but requires something seemingly impossible: a worldly manifestation and practical determinacy. Acting in a purely rational manner, I do the impossible, which is, nevertheless, absolutely necessary. I am compelled to do so. This is possible because I somehow split the realm of phenomena into two by inscribing a different kind of causality into it. The world is thereby not only a natural but also a moral "splace." But to be properly able to perform this action, there is another idea that "coerces my ethical interest": the idea of God, who has created the laws of nature and morality. If I seek to act, I practically (and not theologically) need the idea of the world as God's creation. God then serves as "creator and preserver," as "law giver" and as "judge" of this very world.[33] One cannot think this idea in a purely speculative manner, yet, again, one can comprehend that one cannot comprehend it and thereby also understand its practical necessity.[34] The grounds of morality as well as that which grounds its "splace," namely its creator, cannot be (theoretically) comprehended but nonetheless prove to be necessary for moral practice. They are theoretically impossible and practically necessary. The network of necessary impossibilities gets increasingly complex, and Schmid seeks to demonstrate that we are forced to think this way.

The Conflict of Determinisms: Intelligible Fatalism

What Schmid derives from his argument for God is quite complex. He first states that reason necessarily entails the idea of God, yet the latter remains undeterminable as it is impossible to determine if God exists. "This question remains undecided" because it is theoretically undecidable. Yet, concerning the moral stance toward the world, it is "necessary to decide about this." So, with regard to true morality, *one cannot not decide what cannot be decided* theoretically. One is forced to decide the undecidable.[35] Moral practice is grounded in the necessary although impossible decision of "something" undecidable, of an undecidable existence. Schmid here follows Kant's dictum that "to *orient* oneself in thinking in general terms means: when objective principles of reason are insufficient for holding something to be true, to determine the matter according to a subjective principle."[36] Moral practice begins for Schmid with gaining orientation through a determinate, forced decision. With this decision one is able to do what otherwise seems impossible. The concept of God therefore does also not belong to the theological but to the moral realm. Schmid offers a radical formulation: "We, as moral beings, are not interested in what God in itself is . . . but rather what he is for the world and for us." In this sense, within moral philosophy "God" is the name for this impossible yet necessary decision, which grounds the very existence of moral actions and therefore cannot be a transcendent guarantee. It is irrelevant what he is in himself—and we can never know anyway. The only thing that counts is what he is for us, that is, the placeholder for an impossible yet necessary decision on the existence of morality itself. Through this very act we affirm "an absolute capacity to act (freedom)" precisely because we are forced to do so.[37] We are free when we think we are forced to act rationally and see that to act as a rational being one has to decide the undecidable—with this decision one decides something absolute (God).

It is important to note that the absolute capacity that emerges in this decision is not indeterminate. Since we know its laws, we encounter lawfulness within freedom, a freedom that stands under the law of reason that forced it into existence by compelling it to make the first impossible decision. Or, to render this more dialectically: the absolute capacity to act is itself a limited capacity. First, it is limited because it is an absolute capacity only if this capacity is realized. Thereby the realization lies somehow logically prior to the capacity. It is through the very act of its realization that the capacity retroactively comes into existence. Second, this realization is a forced realization, which implies an additional limitation. A third limitation is an external one, and Schmid expounds it by recourse to determinist theories of action. These limitations are necessary for one simple reason. If we raise the question "Are there laws according to which the actions of the will occur each time or are there none?," we need to answer that the actions of the will are not indeterminate. Only "determinism, which renounces any chance event in nature . . . is the uniquely true and rational philosophy." But what kind of determinism does Schmid defend, then? The kind of freedom he introduced cannot be that of a "mere animal arbitrariness (*arbitrium brutum*)" nor a "free, sensuous arbitrariness (*arbitrium sensitivum liberum*), practical freedom," but clearly must be "moral freedom," a freedom of pure rational actions taking place in this world.[38] Moral freedom is therefore "sensuously applied freedom."[39] If the form of our actions belongs to the realm of phenomena, it must obey its causal order. But with deciding the undecidable, we transformed the world into a moral world. So there are now two kinds of determinism. How can we resolve this "apparent contradiction"? Schmid suggests the following way out: If an agent of an action that occurs in this world refers to itself as an "I," in order for it not to be fully determined by the laws of the world, there must be two "I"s. There must be a split subject involved in morally free actions: an "I" as an object of experience and an "I" as a thing in itself. The former is also an object of inner experiences and representations; the latter is an "unknown I" that grounds the former one and even its modes of representation.[40] The solution of the conflict thus lies in splitting the subject of moral action, splitting determinism into two. In the second edition of his book, Schmid emphasizes that there cannot be a capacity to will evil, not only because this would lead to an "unethical," "gushy [schwärmerischen] fatalism" that he sees at work in Augustine but also because this would make the will into an indifferent capacity that is able to choose. Thereby one would separate the will (as capacity to choose) from moral freedom (which one cannot not choose) and thus from reason (that commands us to choose the way we choose, deciding the undecidable).[41]

But how does this split determinism work if we oppose freedom to heteronomy? What follows from the split between an "I" as thing in itself and the experiential "I" is that only the latter appears within the material world and its historically specific constitution, whereas the former must be thought of as being undetermined by matter but as determining the very form in which matter appears. As matter implies time, the "I" as thing in itself also has to be ultimately timeless. Thus human beings, as embodiments of these two determinisms, are embodiments of a conflict: a conflict in which each side seeks to overdetermine the other; a conflict that exceeds any of our capacities, since it is rather a *conflict of and in capacities*; or, more precisely, a practical conflict between acting in such a way that one realizes, proves, and even constitutes the existence of the capacity of freedom and acting in a way that does not do so. Although reason commands us to act morally, these actions in some sense exceed our conscious grasp. It is, so to speak, not in freedom's (and thus our) hands to determine our actions. There is no metacapacity to decide for or against freedom. *Freedom emerges out of a struggle.* For Schmid freedom is thus always linked to a wager we are forced to make: it is never given, never automatically realized, never granted, not even if it is at the same time considered to be the ultimate capacity of rational beings. But this ultimate capacity is incapable of determining in advance that which knows no metadetermination, namely the conflict of determinisms. There is no determinate ground to their antagonism, although their struggle is absolutely necessary. One cannot determine, and there is no measure to determine, who will win in the conflict of determinisms.

A series of beautiful formulations that Schmid uses in a different context, in a preface to a book by Leonhard Creuzer, can be used to clarify this logic: We have to "risk the strangest of all examples and expose the reader's as well as our own understanding to the thought, which has the particular property of being thinkable only against the necessary laws of reason—the thought of a necessity that is nonnecessity, of an unlimited capacity that is unable to do everything, an incapacity that is the fullest capacity, a complete ground, which does not necessarily ground anything, an individual thing that behaves like a subtracted universal thing, is thus determined and indeterminate; ultimately an independence which results from a double dependence."[42] As freedom is the ultimate capacity, it coincides with absolute incapacity. But this paradox can be thought only by breaking the laws of thought itself, since it designates the limits of reason itself. If one truly thinks that the conflict is the only thing there is, the antagonism of two determinisms (freedom vs. phenomenal embeddedness), their necessary conflict must introduce a fundamental nonnecessity within determinism.

This nonnecessity is *not* identical to freedom as our ultimate capacity but results from the antagonism that human rational beings are doomed to embody. What Schmid calls intelligible fatalism is the thesis that human rational beings cannot avoid this conflict.[43] Precisely because they are embodiments of these two determinisms that come into conflict only because of this very embodiment, there is a contradictory unity of opposites. In other words, the subject of intelligible fatalism is not the result of a trivial dualism. The subject rather emerges from the conflict of two antagonistic determinisms because, as with any antagonism, one can see the necessity of this antagonism only from one of its two sides. Only from the side of reason is one able to think that reason cannot simply resolve the antagonism constitutive of the subject and that freedom will always arise from a struggle to become the overdetermining force within the subject. This is why reason forces one to be an intelligible fatalist. This fatalism entails the crucial insight that the history of all hitherto existing human beings is the history of a struggle for freedom, a struggle to be(come) a subject.

We are determined to never know what will (here and now) result from the persisting conflict, since it exceeds the grasp of our capacity and reason, and we are forced to think this thought, "this unthinkable thought," nonetheless.[44] Reason can be reasonable only if it faces what exceeds its capacity. But there is no blind, mystical, material, or animal fatalism. There is an absolutely necessary intelligible fatalism—a fatalism that "does in no sense destroy reason it its consciousness."[45] It is nonetheless important to not identify the nonknowability and nonnecessity emerging from the antagonistic determinisms with contingency because this would lead to the destruction of rationalism. "There is no chance," and "if we do not want to grant (irrational) chance, there is nothing but necessity."[46] Therefore we know that nonnecessity is absolutely necessary and hence not contingent, although one will never know "the future *obstacles* to self-activity which will limit it in appearance": "The *limits* which constrain rational efficacy are *utterly indeterminable*."[47] To reiterate: this does not mean that freedom is indeterminate. Neither does it mean that transcendental freedom is the only true transcendental. Rather the split of determinisms, the split that is the place of the subject, is the *only* transcendental. A transcendental split, a split transcendental. Therefore the only thing that necessarily remains indeterminate is if the determinable laws of freedom are the determining force in one of the battles of the endless conflict of determinisms. This means that it is not enough to conceive of freedom as a capacity. Rather the very existence of the capacity is proven exclusively through the actions that will have realized it. With this, morality is always at stake, since if phenomenal determinism determines our actions, we do not lose our freedom, but neither does it matter that we "have" freedom. Freedom might be realized (and thus constituted) anytime if we first *accept the struggle* from which it emerges—a struggle we cannot flee from. Here we can derive the fourth slogan for a contemporary provisional morality from Schmid's intelligible fatalism: *Act in such a way that you accept the struggle you cannot flee from!*

Brief Addendum: Kant with Schmid

Two years after the second edition of Schmid's book was published, in 1794, Kant informed the *Berliner Monatsschrift* of his plan to send them an essay that "would be in part distressing to read and in part amusing."[48] It was entitled "The End of All Things." The end of all things—distressing and amusing. Kant therein deals with a thought that "has something horrifying about it because it leads us as it were to the edge of an abyss: for anyone who sinks into it no return is possible . . . and yet there is something attractive there too: for one cannot cease turning his terrified gaze back to it again and again." The end that breaks the endlessly repetitive continuous flow of temporal succession (and is therefore horrifying) is at the same time what generates a compulsion to repeatedly imagine, represent, and return to this temporality. What captures thought is the idea of the end of all things. How can we think this seemingly unthinkable thought? Kant assumes that it must be the "*end of all time* along with the person's uninterrupted duration" and is therefore linked to the idea of a *duratio Noumenon*, a noumenal, ex-temporal duration. This is how the end is internally related to the idea of eternity, for eternity must exceed phenomenal temporal succession, otherwise "the person would indeed never get outside of time."[49] The end (of all things) must thus be linked to the concept of eternity, and the concept of eternity implies the idea of another form of duration, a duration "outside of time," a noumenal duration. Kant here—in a proto-Agambenian move—emphasizes that the end of all things cannot be located within time, since otherwise it would coincide with Judgment Day and, as any day is still part of time, the end of all things would then simply be the last day.[50] The end of all things has to itself be situated out of time, not at the end of time. It is an end outside of that which does not seem to know an end (time). This is why it ends this endless continuation without occurring as one of its successors.

As to why this thought is recurrent, Kant answers by stating that it "must be woven in a wondrous way into universal human reason, because it is encountered among all reasoning peoples at all times." It seems that we move here from the empirical realm to a constitutive feature of reason: it cannot repetitively imagine its own end. One seems to be forced to represent a paradoxical event, an event that coincides with a nonevent, as it ends all temporal events. But, again, why do rational human beings imagine the end of all things? "The ground . . . appears to lie in the fact that reason says to them that the duration of the world has worth only insofar as the rational beings in it conform to the final end of their existence." This is to say, if one were not able to imagine an end, one would be "like a play having no resolution."[51] Without imagining the total end, the total catastrophe, without an act of totalization, it seems there is no end at all and thus no reason. Connecting Kant and Schmid here we can infer the following: If the conflict between the two determinisms lasts endlessly, ultimately this means that its rules are somehow already determined by the phenomenal side, namely endless succession. The conflict is thus not a real conflict, since without the idea of eternity as the overcoming of temporal succession we will always struggle to be truly free, rational, and moral, and thus phenomenality will have always won. This would then simply be our human condition, a condition that ends at some point. And this point is determined by natural causes. To not fall into the trap of embracing human finitude and turning the conflict into another version of the human condition (and hence of anthropology), we cannot but imagine the end of all things—even of this very conflict. This is the only way for reason to reassert itself against the bad infinity of the conflict. This is why imagining the extinction of mankind and reason is a rational thing to do.[52] But the form of this end is important. Since it must be the end of the phenomenal determinism, it therefore must be the end of the conflict, and consequentially also of any possibility to practically realize freedom. So how do I, as a human, rational being, represent from within the conflict itself the end of the conflict that is in my very being and is the only means to establish the conflict properly? Precisely by referring to "the system of the *dualists*, which awards the blessedness to *some* who have been elected, but eternal damnation to all *the rest*." In short, the Lutheran system is the most compelling to reason.[53] Reason must imagine an end of all things, since otherwise we end up turning the struggle of determinisms into a human condition, and we simply revert to an existentialist fatalism. Reason cannot but imagine its own end because it is reason that forces us to comprehend the struggle of determinisms. And this end can be determined either by reason or by phenomenality. It is thus necessary for reason to imagine its own end—and therefore the end of all things. Imagining the end is the fate of reason, and if we cannot pathologize this tendency but must assume it to be absolutely necessary, we have to represent it as the ultimate apocalypse. Hegel will have more to say about this. We can see that rationalism needs the idea of the end (of all things). Even Kant himself therefore might be taken as a constitutive part of rationalism's fatalist history. We also get an additional slogan for contemporary provisional morality: *Act in such a way that you never forget to imagine the end of all things!*

4

Ending with the Worst

Hegel and Absolute Fatalism

If something is it has to be.
—Denis Diderot, *Jacques the Fatalist*

*We arrange [ordnen] it. It breaks down. We
rearrange it and we break down ourselves.*
—Rainer Maria Rilke, *Duino Elegies*

*But the life of Spirit . . . wins its truth only when,
in utter dismemberment, it finds itself.*
—G. W. F. Hegel, *Phenomenology of Spirit*

From the Worst Philosopher . . .

Before the more or less recent revival of a "democratic" or
"Habermasian" Hegel brought about by some of his influen-
tial Anglo-American readers, Hegel was for a very long time
considered to be the worst philosopher, and many of the traditional criticisms are often raised against him even today.[1]
He was considered the worst of all philosophers because with
him thought became the most idealist it could get. His absolute
idealism attempted to reconcile everything in the realm of the
concept, but it started to mystify the real world as his thought
unwillingly flipped over from panlogism to mysticism, and, as
a famous formulation goes, his absolute idealism ultimately

coincided with a "crass materialism."[2] He was too much of an idealist and too much of a materialist.

Hegel's rationalism was deemed untenable in the face of the horrifying and unreasonable historical events that took place after his death. For these events Hegel's famous dictum "The real is the rational, and the rational is the real" did not hold anymore. His emphasis on reason unfolding in history was even accused of being complicit with these unreasonable and violent acts. If Hegel's reason was in fact the only motor of history, this motor ultimately turned out to be a brute force constantly relapsing into barbarism. (We may here think of Adorno and Horkheimer's *Dialectic of Enlightenment*.) Hegel's rationalism thereby produces its own opposite.

Since Hegel saw necessity and reason at work in the world and in history, he defended the unreasonable position that contingency and, with it, concrete contingent individuals do not really play a relevant role in the development of history. Habermas expressed one notable critique of this position in his famous statement "Hegel desires the revolutionizing of reality, without any revolutionaries."[3] Hegel was too much of a rationalist and thereby too much of an irrationalist. He was too dialectical, that is, too systematic. He sought obsessively to integrate everything into an encyclopedic totality, and his method swallowed up everything. His megalomania shows itself in his attempt to consume, by the very means of exclusion, all the things that he excludes.[4] This is why he was, at the same time, too undialectical and too unsystematic, since the idea that everything is dialectically systematizable is itself a highly undialectical idea. Dialectics cannot be all there is, otherwise there would be no dialectical relation between dialectical totality and that which must be its determinate negation. Hence there never can be a completely dialectical system. In short,

Hegel was too much of a dialectician and thereby too much of a nondialectician.

He was also said to be too much of an eschatological thinker, overgeneralizing the Christian Trinitarian logic and applying it to everything. Consequently he universalized a reconciliatory religious narrative in which everything, even revelation itself, becomes transparent and can be understood in an a priori fashion such that predictions about the unfolding of history can be made. This alleged eschatological thread haunted Hegel-oriented Marxism up to Stalin, as if it were a chronic conceptual illness that grounded the illusory belief in the stable laws of historical progress toward an ultimate good (i.e., communism). Yet this eschatological strand ultimately prevented people from properly engaging the concrete demands of the concrete world and produced a bad kind of fatalism, in which everything always already seems predetermined. For "if the revolution is inevitable, why do we have to work for it?"[5] This ultimately boils down to the thesis that Hegel presupposed the absolute from the very beginning—a criticism shared by thinkers such as Nietzsche and Heidegger. The critique that Hegel was too eschatological means that he simply presupposed what he tried to expound. But, for the very same reason, Hegel was also criticized for being too antieschatological, as he foreclosed the possibility of intervening in the world. He always overemphasized what *is* at the expense of what *ought to be*. Therefore he did not have to say anything about the future—a temporal dimension that allegedly plays no role in Hegel whatsoever—and became an apologist of the status quo.[6] He was a thinker without any redeeming perspective. Because of his way of conceptualizing freedom's unfolding in history, Hegel, as the philosopher of freedom, prevents us from thinking freedom properly. His position thereby seems to confirm that the idea of progressive development, as Lacan once stated, "is merely a hypothesis of mastery."[7] Hegel, as the philosopher of freedom, is also the philosopher of unfreedom.

Even this brief overview of criticisms shows that for a long time Hegel was, and maybe in many aspects still is, philosophy's bête noire, the worst. In this peculiar contest only Plato might be a true competitor. Hegel is the worst because he is somehow too much: too much of everything (reason, logic, revelation, freedom, etc.), too much of the opposite of everything, too much of nothing, so to speak. Hegel is "too much of too much."[8] It is as if his thought exemplified a peculiar version of Russell's famous antinomy in which any answer to the problem necessarily also leads to subscribing to its opposite. Although he is commonly accepted as a thinker of contradiction, his thought itself seems to embody a peculiar excess of contradiction—not in the sense that he deals with too many contradictions at once but in the sense that there is too much contradiction in the Hegelian system (of contradictions) itself. Is it therefore really surprising that Hegel, the thinker of freedom and reason, is ultimately a fatalist? Maybe even an absolute one? What if we just have to change our perspective slightly? What if the "too muchness" of Hegel is not a flaw but rather a strength, which therefore also provides the most robust account of the constitutive link between freedom and fatalism? We may just recall some of the crucial categories on which Hegel relies to unfold his conception of freedom, and we will immediately see that nearly all of them are supposedly discredited today: totality, teleology, necessity, closure, completion, system, absolute idea, absolute knowing, and, last but not least, the end, for example, of art, history, or philosophy. These concepts alone show why Hegel still today might be considered the worst. Indeed if there ever was one, Hegel was certainly *the* philosopher of the end. Everyone knows that he is supposed to have declared the end of history as well as the end of art, politics, religion, and, ultimately, philosophy.[9] We can draw a conclusion here that might appear obvious, but it can demonstrate the inherent link between Hegel and fatalism: Hegel is not only the worst of all philosophers, but his philosophy cannot but be a philosophy of the worst, a philosophy that declares the very end of everything and of all human practices. Although this is an obvious possibility, it did not occur to many readers of Hegel. Hegel's philosophy of reason and freedom should be read as an argument for the kind of fatalism that assumes the worst. In Hegel there is no real freedom without assuming the worst, and this is a fully rational assumption.

To the Philosophy of the Worst . . .

We should start by returning to some of the passages where Hegel discusses the emergence of philosophy. One such passage can be found in his *Lectures on the History of Philosophy*:

> Philosophy first commences when a race [*ein Volk*] for the most part has left its concrete life, when separation and change of class have begun, and the people approach toward their fall; when a gulf has arisen between inward strivings and external reality, and the old forms of Religion, &c., are no longer satisfying; when Mind manifests its indifference to its living existence or rests unsatisfied therein, and moral life becomes dissolved. Then it is that Mind that takes refuge in the clear space of thought to create for itself a kingdom of thought in opposition to the world of actuality, and Philosophy is the reconciliation following upon the destruction of that real world which thought has begun.[10]

Philosophy is the reconciliation that follows the destruction brought about by thought itself. Therefore philosophy is not reconciliation that overcomes destruction but reconciliation with destruction. Philosophy emerges only when decay has already begun and is unstoppable, inevitable, and thus necessary. Philosophy thinks this necessary decay. It thinks that the end has already happened, and it is simply waiting for its actualization. It begins when there is indifference in the world and in spirit. And there is indifference in the world when there is an inevitable decline of the understanding of freedom, a gulf between what I think I can do and the reality of my action. Indifference is a sign of unpreventable decay, and philosophy emerges as thought of this destruction, because of this destruction. More precisely there is philosophical thought only because the world is destructive and destroyed, and philosophy is the form of thought that thinks the annihilation and disappearance of the world. Philosophy therefore cannot but be the philosophy of the end. Only in this way can it begin.[11] This is also how the concrete shape of spirit emerges within history: its "accomplishment is at the same time its dissolution [*sein Untergang*], and the rise of another spirit."[12] If we take this claim as a depiction of the very structure of the emergence of spirit, it becomes clear that spirit as such emerges from dissolution. Philosophy as the highest form of spirit must therefore follow the same logic.

There is no spirit without dissolution, and spirit is the very spirit of its own dissolution. But therefore spirit is more than just dissolution. The thought of dissolution does not only emerge from dissolution itself but is also *the thought of this very dissolution in dissolution*. It is "the restoration of its principles from the ruin to which they had been brought" by thinking this very ruin. This is the general logic of spirit: "It certainly makes war upon itself—consumes its own existence; but in the very destruction it works up that existence into a new form . . . working on which it exalts itself to a new grade." Spirit works through its own destruction, and thereby it becomes its own vanishing material. This is why philosophy cannot be only the philosophy of history, since there is no history without spirit's war on itself, without the loss of spirit. As we can see, the thought of the logic as well as of the history of spirit originates in spirit's dissolution and dismemberment. If philosophy is the philosophy of spirit, it also has to take into account the very "nature" of spirit. This nature is that "Spirit, in rendering itself objective and making this its being an object of thought, on the one hand destroys the determinate form of its being, on the other hand gains a comprehension of the universal element which it involves, and thereby gives a new form to its inherent principle." There is no spirit without destruction, and philosophy, as a part of spirit and the philosophy of spirit, must take into account not only that the result of spirit's process is destruction of old forms and the creation of a new form but also that it "is essentially the result of its own activity." Spirit's concrete manifestation follows this logic: it produces something, yet its "fruit does not fall back into the bosom of the people that produced and matured it; on the contrary, it becomes a poison-draught to it. That poison-draught it cannot let alone, for it has an insatiable thirst for it: the taste of the draught is its annihilation, though at the same time the rise of a new principle."[13] Each form of spirit generates something that it compulsively desires, yet it is precisely that which will bring it down.

If philosophy "has to do with the *eternally present*," it must take the very logic of spirit as its object, as any concrete form of spirit is nothing but a particular element of its own destruction.[14] But this also means that any philosophy as philosophy of spirit begins from spirit's general annihilation and is nonetheless a peculiar shape of spirit. There is no philosophy of history without the destruction of all possible determinate forms of spirit that give rise to the philosophy of history. Philosophy can begin only when spirit's history has come to an end and this end is thought. In this sense "philosophy in any case always comes on the scene too late . . . only when actuality has completed its process of formation and attained its finished state."[15] The finished state is the state of its end. Philosophy as philosophy of spirit is necessarily the form spirit adopts when it seeks to grasp not only one of its particular dissolution and destruction but also the dissolution of itself as such. This is why one of its highest forms is the philosophy of the history of philosophy. As philosophy of spirit, philosophy of history, and philosophy of the history of philosophy, philosophy is philosophy of the dissolution, of the destruction, and of the annihilation of spirit. Therefore the history of spirit is a "slaughter-bench," not only of individuals but also of spirit itself.[16] Yet if this is the general principle of the practical realization of spirit, we are not dealing with a simple history of progress, as is often claimed, but with a peculiar kind of worsening that should not be misunderstood as a gradual development. Rather we can say that things get worse and worse simply because this *is* spirit. Spirit is worsening. If there is progress, it is progress within the history of worsening.

Of course this conclusion does not simply mean that things go progressively down the drain. Rather it suggests that all history is necessarily, on a structural level, the end of history. Historical unfolding is nothing more than the destruction of previous historical unfolding. But this conclusion is not simply a praise of destruction but rather implies that the proper concept of history and the end of history must become indistinguishable. The concept of the history of spirit and the concept of the dissolution of spirit must be one and the same. This is consistent with Hegel's famous passage about the movement of philosophical thought from the end of the preface to the *Philosophy of Right*: "When philosophy paints its grey in grey, then has a shape of life grown old. By philosophy's grey in grey it cannot be rejuvenated but only understood. The owl of Minerva begins its flight only with the falling of dusk."[17] Philosophy begins when a shape of life begins to decay, when it has grown old and is on the verge of dying. This means not only, as Robert Pippin has rightly argued, that Hegel does not present any normative account of what a state or a civil society should look like, but that he depicts the status quo of his contemporary society because it is a shape of life grown old that has come close to its end.[18]

Philosophy, especially Hegel's philosophy depicting what is and never what ought to be, can therefore never become apologetic. It depicts what is in a state of decline, and it can depict it only because it is in this very decline. The end is therefore not only near but also always already here. *If there is philosophy, the end has always already taken place.* For a philosophy that itself claims to entail the general concept of philosophy, as Hegel's philosophy contends, this must mean that everything has always already come to an end. In short, for Hegel everything is always already lost, and the end has always already arrived, or the apocalypse has always already taken place.[19]

To read Hegel as an apocalyptic thinker is certainly not a new idea. Already Jacob Taubes has argued that Hegel's thought, especially the idea of an end of history, is closely linked to the eschatology of Joachim of Floris.[20] Karl Löwith pointed out that Hegel "displaces the Christian expectation of the end of the world of time into the course of the world process, and the absolute of faith into the rational realm of history."[21] For Taubes and Löwith, Hegel is the philosopher of the revelation of all things within the world, and the medium of this revelation is history. Therefore Hegel is an apocalyptic thinker since revelation must imply the idea of things coming to an end. More recently Malcolm Bull called Hegel "the most apocalyptic of philosophers" because in Hegel there is what he defines as "apocalyptic," that is, "the revelation of contradiction or indeterminacy."[22] He treats Hegel as a thinker not of the revelation of ultimate harmony but of unavoidable contradiction and inescapable indetermination inscribed into reason and freedom. Hegel is read as if he were Schmid. What these readings share is that they all assume that Hegel is a thinker of progress: of progressive revelation either of things becoming ultimately transparent or of things ultimately showing their indeterminate and contradictory face. Therefore the progress at stake here cannot have anything to do with a Kantian regulative idea that one endlessly approximates. It is of course true for Hegel that "Reason is not content with an approximation which, as something 'neither cold nor hot,' it will 'spew out of its mouth.'"[23] Yet to comprehend the specificity of Hegel's absolute fatalism, we should recall his fundamental Lutheran commitment. He once wrote, "I am a Lutheran, and through philosophy been at once completely confirmed in Lutheranism."[24] He also famously stated, "What began with Luther as faith in [the form of] feeling and the witness of spirit, is precisely what spirit, since become more mature, has striven to apprehend in the *concept* in order to free itself, and so to find itself, in the present."[25] So what can we make of these claims?

To Philosophical . . .

Is Hegel faithful to Luther's idea of predestination and divine providence? Could the concepts of necessity, teleology, systematicity, completion, and the end be aligned to formulate a Lutheran position in philosophy? And what would such a position be like? Before these questions can be dealt with, we have to note that a certain danger appears here. Because of all the emphasis on the end one might be tempted to read Hegel as a philosopher of finitude, which is clearly neither a properly dialectical reading nor especially appropriate to Hegel's self-understanding. Therefore it is important to stress that Hegel's emphasis on the end does not lead us back to the finitude of all things, human beings, practices, and so on. It also does not lead us to the supposedly more complex conception of limitedness that acknowledges that although all our striving for the absolute will finally be in vain as we will never be able to attain it, we are still not able not to strive as this is inscribed into our very nature. If this were in fact Hegel's ultimate point, we could understand this very structure as the meaning of "absolute knowing." This understanding would then ultimately enable us to laugh at not being able to let go of our pretentious goals and would teach us not to take ourselves too seriously.[26] In such a reading Hegel would ultimately be a cynic.

The conceptual reason that Hegel is not simply a thinker of finitude and limitedness is linked to the fact that philosophy does not emerge when a particular finite shape of spirit disappears. He does not argue that what philosophy shows us is that all shapes of spirit are finite. By assuming such a position we would still rely on at least one thing that we—in most cases unwillingly—postulate as not finite, namely finitude itself. If everything were finite, then finitude itself would become a transhistorical category. Hegel's philosophy avoids the assumption of any stable transhistorical or transcendental ground and radicalizes the idea of finitude itself, so that philosophy proper emerges only when finitude as such is also dissolved. If this provides the groundless ground for Hegel's philosophy of freedom, at least three things are clear: (1) Freedom cannot be a capacity, since all capacities must be realized and are always already exhausted and dissolved when the true freedom of spirit emerges. Philosophy thus cannot be a philosophy of capacities (and therefore cannot be Aristotelian), as it emerges only when everything we are capable of has already vanished. (2) Hegel's absolute fatalism is more subtractive than any subtractive endeavor encountered before in the history of philosophical rationalism because it does not rely on any stable ground anymore but rather springs from the very process of the vanishing of all things. Its most fundamental move is the conceptualization of the end. Hegel's absolute fatalism therefore identifies the moment when there must be a vanishing even of the process of concrete vanishings. (3) If philosophy always arrives too late and the apocalypse has always already taken place, the only thing that Hegel's absolute fatalism can reveal is that there is nothing to reveal. Hegel's thought is thus not about what is "to come" but about what is "always already gone"—which for Hegel is a precondition for freedom. But the whole question is how to conceive of this nothing that is revealed when there is nothing to be revealed. Against this background, how can we make sense of predestination and providence?

Providence . . .

The concept of providence implies that history has already reached its end. In his *Encyclopedia*, Hegel has the following to say with regard to providence:

> What underlies the thought of divine providence will turn out for us subsequently to be the concept. This is the truth of necessity and contains the latter as sublated in itself just as, conversely, necessity in itself is the concept. Necessity is blind only insofar as it is not comprehended and there is, therefore, nothing more wrong than the reproach of a blind fatalism, a charge made against the philosophy of history, because it regards its task to be the knowledge of the necessity of what has happened. The philosophy of history acquires thereby the meaning of a theodicy, and, while there are those who believe themselves to be honouring the divine providence by excluding necessity from it, by this abstraction they in fact degrade it to a blind, arbitrary choice devoid of reason. . . . God knows what he wants and, in his eternal will, he is not determined by inner or outer chance, instead bringing about, without resistance, what he wants.[27]

It is thus not only the case that philosophy articulates in the medium of the concept that which Luther articulated in terms of feeling; much more, the concept itself *is* providence. In a crucial passage of the *Science of Logic*, Hegel states that the concept of essence as such—that is, reflection in and of itself—is "to be within itself the absolute recoil upon itself."[28] Thus it must also hold that the essence of the concept must be within itself the absolute recoil upon itself. What does this mean? In the present context it means that we first move from the idea of providence to the concept of providence, and thereby it becomes clear that the concept is the only providence there is. Any "progression toward a result is thus at the same time a returning into itself, a recoil into itself upon itself that is in itself its own self-recoiling. It is what was described above as the true nature of spirit."[29] It is in the nature of spirit that also the concept of providence must entail an absolute recoil of the concept of providence within the concept of providence, an absolute recoil within the concept of absolute necessity upon the concept of absolute necessity. These formulas, however, seem to make things more opaque. We moved from the concept of providence to the concept itself being providence. But to clarify this, let's shift our perspective once again.

If for Hegel philosophy is "a justification of providence,"[30] it must be a defense of absolute necessity. Assuming that there is a "plan of Providence" ensures that "there is Reason in history"— and thus not only contingent events.[31] Assuming that there is providence enables us to uphold a rationalist position. Otherwise things would happen for merely arbitrary reasons or for no reason at all, which would defy any attempt to comprehend them. If there were pure chance events in the world, there would paradoxically be no chance but only blind fatalism. Blind fatalism emerges as soon as we claim that things happen without a possible explanation, so we confront something that defies comprehensibility and leads us necessarily into heteronomous determination. The idea of pure chance entails within itself an absolute recoil upon itself, and it turns out to be just another name for blind fatalism. If there were no reason in history, there would not be sheer contingency but rather mere fatalism. Therefore we need to start by assuming absolute necessity because only in this way can we get to something other than absolute necessity. This is why we need a justification of providence. Taking up a fundamentally Cartesian move, no matter how counterintuitive it may sound, we could argue that this justification is not an apology but the only way to true freedom and contingency. But necessity alone is not enough. One also needs what Kant already saw as a necessity for and of reason, namely the idea of the end of all things, that is, the idea of totality. Necessity thereby implies totality, and this is why Hegel speaks also of "the totality of reason."[32] Reason needs to totalize itself, otherwise there is no absolute necessity and hence no reason in history. This also means that in this very move reason totalizes its own nature, the movement of absolute recoil that it is. Thus, as we will see later, it also de-totalizes itself. As a result rationalism needs absolute necessity and the idea of totality, and obviously these two concepts constitute the concept of divine providence. This concept will then internally invert into the providence of the concept, which will turn out to be the very precondition of freedom, contingency, and so on. But initially this is just another way of asserting that there is no rationalism without universalism and no universalism without rationalism.

Modifying Hegel's famous claim that evil resides in the very gaze that perceives evil all around, we can thus conclude that absolute necessity and providence reside in the very gaze that perceives necessity and providence all around. Just as the clarity of Scripture in Luther depended on the right spirit, reason in history depends on the right, rationalist spirit that sees reason in history. Reason thus depends on itself. Hegel's formula for this is the following: "To him who looks upon the world rationally, the world in its turn presents a rational aspect. The relation is mutual."[33] The ground from which we see what we seek to see is a groundless ground, which again shows that philosophy has no stable foundation to rely upon: with its very emergence, the ground from which philosophy emerged has always already vanished. Against this background, what can we do with the passages in Hegel's *Philosophy of History* where he clearly states that in certain periods of time nothing of any importance seems to have happened? Certainly, empirically, things have happened. To resolve this paradox we should draw the following conclusion: There are also mere chance events in history. But mere chance events immediately regress to a blind fatalism. In this sense chance events in history are not true historical events but blind repetitions of what there is. They are not manifestations of absolute necessity or spirit, since it is spirit's nature to invert itself internally. These blind events can be in an absolutely necessary way derived from the concept of chance, that is, from blind fatalism, which at the same time is of no interest to reason since it is what lacks reason. This is also why there is no philosophy in those times, which means that those times did not properly apprehend themselves in the form of thought (and the concept).

Yet in light of these discussions, what are we to make of the claim that philosophy can become the philosophy of history only if it is the justification of providence? It is at first crucial to distinguish between the religious belief in providence, as in Luther, and the philosophical use of this concept. In Luther it was absolutely crucial for predestination to be unknowable to produce the salutary dimension of despair that prepared the advent of true faith. It was thus necessary to comprehend that one would never be able to comprehend God's motives or his plan. In philosophy, however, it is necessary to know what is absolutely necessary, that is, to know providence. Hegel already contended in his *Science of Logic* that the task of this science is to expose "God as he is in his eternal essence before the creation of nature and a finite mind."[34] For philosophy it is necessary to counter "the *doctrine* that it is impossible to know God." God is knowable, and so is his plan. The latter is not discussed in the *Science of Logic* but is exposed in its necessary totality in *The Philosophy of History*. This is why the latter "is the true *Theodicaea*, the justification of God in History. . . . [It] is not only not 'without God,' but essentially His Work." So God and his plan and work are systematically linked because of the following logical structure: Even if God precedes creation, we can think him only after the act of creation has been completed. God in himself before the creation can be thought only when we think him after the creation and, thus, after the realization of his plan. There is no God without creation. There is God before the creation, but he remains unthinkable. There is thus no thinkable God without his plan and its realization. This is why *The Philosophy of History* can claim, "The final aim is God's purpose with the world; but God . . . can, therefore, will nothing other than himself—his own Will."[35] God's will is thus the first and most fundamental "free will that wills itself."[36] God's plan for the world is ultimately directed at himself: the progression toward a result is, at the same time, a returning to itself, God's return back to God. God's plan is to make himself thinkable, to will his own willing. Yet we may here raise the question: Where does the self-recoiling occur in this context? To answer this question, we need to take a step back: we can think God before the creation only after the creation, and therefore "we have to take the latter as it is."[37] We have to take creation as it is because it is the manifestation of God's will (that is, his plan) and must therefore be absolutely necessary. What does it mean for something to be absolutely necessary? As Hegel states in the *Logic*, "The absolutely necessary only *is* because it *is*; it otherwise has neither condition nor ground. . . . *It is, therefore, because it is*."[38] The absolutely necessary is unconditional and groundless, and if God's plan cannot be thought without its creation, its creation must be absolutely necessary.

This means that we have to take *what* is as it is and take it *as* it is precisely *because* it is *what* it is. This is how we assume that "God governs the world," and "the actual working of his government—the carrying out of his plan—is the History of the World."[39] But here things get complicated: if God can be thought, he must be thought as being absolutely necessary because there can be no condition and no ground for him. This already shows that the absolutely necessary coincides with and is indistinguishable from absolute freedom and therefore absolute contingency (as in Descartes). At the same time, it is also true that God can be thought as preceding his creation only on the condition that there is a creation. But this means that God is conditioned by it and thus not absolutely necessary anymore. Yet if his plan must also be taken to be absolutely necessary (if reason lies in the way things are because they are absolutely necessarily the way they are), then there can be no ground or condition for this plan. But if the plan is God's plan, how could it not be grounded in and thus conditioned by God? And if this were to be the case, the plan also would not be absolutely necessary anymore since there would be a ground conditioning it, namely God. We can see here an effect of the recoiling implied by the concept of providence. A strange twofold contradiction emerges: If God's plan is absolutely necessary, it cannot and at the same time nonetheless must have God as its condition. And if God must be *thought* as absolutely necessary, he cannot and at the same cannot but depend on his plan, that is, on his creation. By assuming the absolute necessity of God and his plan, we seem to lose the absolute necessity of both. They are mutually conditioning and hence do not seem to be unconditional. How to resolve this apparent deadlock? Here the true and absolute recoiling move comes to the fore. The absolutely necessary consequence of this deadlock of absolute necessity and obvious impossibility of God and his plan is that *the only divine plan there is is that there is no divine plan.*

In the End God Had to Admit

Hegel states, "Our earnest endeavor must be directed to the recognition of the ways of Providence, the means it uses, and the historical phenomena in which it manifests itself; and we must show their connection with the general principle [of freedom] above mentioned."[40] In order to understand and know God's plan, we need a concrete analysis of concrete providential situations. This analysis follows an "imperative" that we can find in Hegel's *Logic*: we have to "take up what is before us [*aufzunehmen, was vorhanden ist*]."[41] So we take up what is as that which it is and thus think God's plan. But from the perspective of philosophy, what is it that is before us? If philosophy begins only when a figure of spirit has grown old, and if God's plan can be thought only when it is revealed in its totality (otherwise there could be no philosophy of history), it must necessarily follow that the totality of what is before us is a vanishing totality. This is another way of stating that there is philosophy of history as the determinate presentation of divine providence only at the end of history. Here we can see the absolute recoil of the concept within and upon itself: the concept of divine providence implies that it must itself be vanishing. The fact that God's plan can be thought only if it has vanished in its totality proves this plan to be absolutely necessary.

Consequently the philosophy of history can properly emerge only at the end of this process, when even God's plan and with it everything that is has already vanished. It can emerge only if the end has already taken place. One should therefore read literally what Hegel states in the preface to *The Philosophy of History*: that "this 'Idea' or 'Reason' is the *True*, the *Eternal*, the absolutely *powerful* essence; that it reveals itself in the World, and that in that World nothing is revealed but this."[42] In German, Hegel's formulation entails an ambiguity, namely that in that world nothing (*Nichts*) is revealed *als sie*, which one can read in two ways: nothing is revealed in the world but reason, or nothing is the very form in which reason is revealed. We should—in a Hegelian spirit—read both of them together: in the world, God's creation, nothing is revealed but reason, but reason is revealed in the world precisely as the nothing of revelation. In different terms, *the only thing that is revealed*—which *is* reason—*is that nothing is revealed. But this is a revelation.* This structure is what Hegel's concept of the cunning of reason is about. Slavoj Žižek rightly remarked, "The Hegelian Cunning of Reason . . . is not that Reason is a secret force behind the scenes using human agents for its purposes: there are *nothing but* agents following their particular purposes, and what they do 'auto-poetically' organizes itself into a larger pattern."[43]

We can see here that Hegel's cunning maneuver concerning divine providence consists in staying faithful to Luther by inverting him in a specific way. The point is not that providence is ungraspable. It is fully graspable. But when one grasps it, one comprehends that there is nothing to be grasped. This nothing is a fully determinate nothing. And therefore it is not simply nothing. It is somehow more than nothing. If everything that happened must have happened because God willed it, and if everything that ever happened became *properly thinkable only when it vanished*, God's whole plan is a plan of vanishing, a vanishing plan, and thus the plan is that *in the end* there is no plan. God's plan does not entail a hidden message to be deciphered. Or better: the only message to be deciphered is that there is no message to be deciphered. Providence can be properly comprehended when it is comprehended in its vanishing totality, that is, by philosophy. This does not simply mean that we can understand God's thoughts from before the creation only after the creation, but that we can understand them only after the complete vanishing of creation itself. The argument seems tautological, yet it is not: after the vanishing of creation, which is what is before us as creation, we ultimately end where we began, before the creation. This is Hegel's tribute to Luther's idea that we have to put ourselves in the position of being before the creation of mankind, since only in this way can we stop willing and act as if we did not exist.[44] We can think God before the creation only after the vanishing of the vanishing creation.

It is important to add here yet another recoiling move. What are we actually thinking when, after the vanishing of creation, we think God's thoughts from before the creation? The answer is we think his predestined plan. Yet this predestined plan is that there is no predestined plan. This is why Hegel can justifiably claim that "the great assumption that what has taken place on this side, in the world, has also done so in conformity with reason—which is what first gives the history of Philosophy its true interest—is nothing else than trust in Providence, only in another form."[45] This *other form* that amounts to a slight shift of perspective completely changes everything. This shift makes clear that God's plan can be known, but knowing it does not help at all as this very knowledge is ultimately a knowledge that there is nothing to know. To completely know divine providence thus means that we know something, but this knowledge amounts to knowing nothing. Yet it is still more than not knowing anything. In the same vein Hegel claims, "What experience and history teach is this—that peoples and governments never have learned anything from history." *The lesson of the philosophy of history is that there is no lesson from the philosophy of history, and this is an important lesson.* This is why Hegel can contend that ultimately reason is "its own material which it commits to its own Active Energy to work up."[46] Therefore Hegel's ultimate punch line is that understanding God's plan means understanding that the only plan is that there is no plan. Yet, and this is the next step in the recoiling movement of divine providence, that which is mediated through negation—knowing through history that God's plan is that there is no plan—finally coincides with immediacy.

The coincidence of mediation and immediacy leads us to the necessary insight that God has no plan other than the plan to have no plan, which ultimately amounts to having no plan. First, we have to assume that we can think God before the creation only after the creation. His creation reveals that there is nothing to be revealed and that there is no plan. This providential detour proves that the only providence there is must be that there is no providence. But because of the coincidence of mediation (the plan that there is no plan) and immediacy (this means there is no plan), ultimately *God himself has to admit that he has no plan.*

But if he himself must necessarily admit that he has no plan (and who but God should have a plan since his concept entails the idea of omnipotence and providence?), this means that *God himself has to admit that he does not exist. And this is absolutely necessary.* Thereby the very fulfillment of his plan in the end leads to the self-abolition of God. This is the absolute recoil. If God knows that "no matter how well-planned things are, somehow they will go wrong" and that eventually everything goes wrong, it is because of this very knowledge that even God is forced to admit that there is no God.[47] The structure of this knowledge is what Hegel in his *Phenomenology of Spirit* grasps under the name of absolute knowing.[48] Its paradoxical structure necessarily entails not only that one knows that there is no God but also that God too knows that he himself does not exist and that he admits it.

Hegel's philosophy of history demonstrates that God has to die, but he has to die twice, both as son (as his providential plan) and as father (as the planner). The first death occurs within his creation (as Christ), which means that creation is nothing but a vanishing series of vanishing moments. When Christ dies ("Father, why have you forsaken me?"), we can necessarily infer that God himself for a moment becomes an atheist and doubts his own existence. And ultimately, after the whole unfolding of history, he has to admit that he does not exist. So things get continuously worse. Not only does providence consist in the vanishing of providence itself, but God must admit both that he has no plan and that he does not even exist (and therefore his plan cannot exist either). God himself has to admit that he does not exist. Could things be more apocalyptic or more fatalistic than this? But one can see that this form of absolute fatalism or of fatalism of the absolute is at the same time not only fully rationalist but also the very precondition of a true philosophy of freedom. For if God has no plan and must admit that he does not exist, we have to assume that the worst, the apocalypse, has always already happened, precisely *because it happened even before the creation of the world and of history.* (After all, God admitted that he did not exist then either.) This is where an absolute rationalist and an absolute fatalist, that is Hegel, locates the very origin of freedom. Freedom is not something that we have in our possession; it is not a capacity; it is not something; and it is not even nothing. It is located where there is even less than nothing, where the apocalypse has always already happened, before the creation of nature, time, and any finite mind. What preposterous consequences! Even comic, aren't they?

Absolute Knowing, Absolute Fatalism

Real comedy begins with and in reason. Rebecca Comay has suggested that for Hegel "the ultimate obstacles to reason are those generated by reason." We encounter here a peculiar parallax. For not only is it fully rational to assume absolute necessity (which leads to the assumption of an absolute fatalism and of a fatalism of the absolute whose fundamental proposition is that the apocalypse has always already happened), but because of the very structure of reason itself, it is also absolutely necessary that reason cannot simply assume its own rational(ist) insight. Reason is inventive and invents infinite ways of resisting the assumption of a truly rational position. So things get worse after the worst has always already happened. Reason constantly invents new ways of resisting what it must think. It constantly shies away from what it has to confront. I take Comay to suggest that it is precisely the movement generated by this paradoxical structure of reason that Hegel in his *Phenomenology of Spirit* depicts: reason struggling with itself, seeking to resist its own absolutely necessary insight, endlessly inventing new means of resisting it, and thereby endlessly staging that the worst always already did take place and it keeps getting worse. Hegel's philosophy grasps this very self-recoiling movement of reason, and it therefore is, in Comay's words, "like driving with both the brake and the accelerator pedal down at once. To think philosophically is to dash again and again against the same wall, digging the same hole, skipping and turning like a stuck record, forever repeating."[49] Somehow it seems rational to resist the insight that is absolutely reasonable. One has to resist it, but one cannot resist it either. The situation is exactly like Kant's description of the end of all things: it is terrifying, yet one cannot look away.

If Hegel's *Phenomenology*, which he himself conceived of as the necessary precondition for his philosophical project, depicts a seemingly endless series of resistances of reason against its own absolutely necessary insight, then the *Phenomenology* must present a series of vanishing resistances against what is absolutely necessary from which new resistances arise. Alenka Zupančič perspicaciously remarked that many of the chapter titles of the *Phenomenology* read as if they were titles of comedies, and now one can see why.[50] So how do we interpret the most contested element of Hegel's thought: absolute knowing? Do absolute fatalism and absolute comedy also coincide?

As I already demonstrated, absolute knowing appears precisely when the movement of vanishing itself vanishes. If vanishing means that things come to an end and are fully externalized, the vanishing of vanishing must be an internalization of this very movement of externalization, what Hegel calls the "recollection, the *inwardizing* [*Er-innerung*], of that experience." Reason knows and thus assumes its own vanishing resistances against its own insight that everything has always already vanished. In absolute knowing, reason assumes its own absolute necessity. It thus takes itself *as* it is and assumes that the insight that the apocalypse has always already happened is not simply a rational and reasonable claim, but in a very precise sense it *is* reason. When reason takes itself as what it is, it assumes that the worst has always already happened. This is the very constitution of reason, as Hegel puts it, the "Calvary of absolute Spirit." It appears, then, that reason is truly reason only when it sacrifices reason. It is therefore interesting that Hegel himself utilizes the language of sacrifice when speaking about absolute knowing: "To know one's limit is to know how to sacrifice oneself."[51]

Absolute knowing is the knowledge of one's own limit, which entails that one knows how to sacrifice oneself. What does this mean? All the stages of the *Phenomenology* seek to find a stable stopping point for substance, for the subject, and for knowledge itself. They represent ways of clinging to some stability, which ultimately proves to be a way for reason to resist its own insight. The very idea of stability is unsustainable. Reason cannot escape the conclusion that there is nothing to cling to, and this knowledge is continually brought about by the very attempts to escape it. But, as we have already seen, we may know that knowledge is fundamentally unstable, but this knowledge is not enough for absolute knowing to be absolute.[52] The insight into the instability of knowledge is what we cannot assume. Accepting that knowledge cannot know and thus integrate what it cannot assume constitutively implies that knowledge knows that in it there is something that it cannot know because it is what makes knowledge itself impossible. Absolute knowing knows this, and it knows that it knows something that simply cannot be known. It is an impossible knowledge that knows the limits of knowledge. Therefore it knows how to sacrifice knowledge. It is a knowledge about giving up knowledge, about letting go of it. Without this impossible knowledge, we could not know what we know, namely that knowledge is constitutively limited because it always seeks to flee what it knows.

Absolute knowing stops the flight of reason against its own rational insight, yet it does not arrest movement. Rather it makes it possible for us to hand ourselves over to another kind of movement. Absolute knowing is the knowledge of the impossibility of assuming an absolutely necessary rational insight. Therefore it is also absolutely necessary knowledge. Absolute knowing is not an objective knowledge of something or of the absolute. Neither is it the knowledge of an object that may be called the absolute, which is a traditional misreading of Hegel. Rather absolute knowing is a knowledge that knows what is constitutive of any knowledge: it is based on something that it cannot integrate into itself. I simply cannot assert that whose assertion would make it impossible in the first place for me to assert it. But this is exactly what absolute knowing asserts.

It is therefore the point where the vanishing itself vanishes. Absolute knowing is absolute comedy: I am assuming what I cannot assume because it would make the place from which I can assume it impossible. Yet the impossible is, as shown, absolutely necessary. With absolute knowing I attain a (position in and with regard to) knowledge that is necessary and impossible. But precisely for this reason absolute knowing sacrifices knowledge.

As Hegel states in the *Science of Logic*, absolute knowing is so pure that it "ceases itself to be knowledge."[53] Why? Because this knowledge is knowingly assuming what makes knowledge itself impossible and incomplete. To put it differently, truth emerges from this instability, the unavoidable and necessary vacillation of knowledge. More precisely, the instability *is* the truth of knowledge because it is what exceeds knowledge. It cannot be integrated into knowledge, because in that case it would be simply a form of knowledge. So absolute knowing is a knowledge that knows that there is something it knows that it cannot assume as its own knowledge. It knows that it does not know that it knows. Absolute knowing is therefore *unknowing*. It does know that it has a knowledge that it does not know it has because it cannot assume it. Nevertheless it still assumes it, and with this move it knows that the worst has always already happened and that it even got worse afterward, since one cannot assume this absolutely necessary fact. Hegel's ultimate dialectical torsion is that absolute knowing *is* the full assumption of that which one cannot assume within knowledge. This is why it knows how to sacrifice knowledge. It is thus real knowledge because it entails an assertion of the *Real* of knowledge, the sacrifice of knowledge within knowledge. In short, it is truth itself. This truth emerges as an outcome of an absolute fatalism, a fatalism that is absolute. This also means that only through absolute fatalism can we distinguish truth from knowledge.

Absolute knowing is absolute fatalism. Or more precisely: the ab-solute is fatalism, fatalism is ab-solute.

First as Fatalism of Substance, Then as Fatalism of the Subject

What does all this mean for the critique of the identification of freedom with a human capacity? Is Hegel ultimately nothing but an apologist for the present state of things? No, Hegel's absolute fatalism is the very precondition of preparing for that for which we cannot prepare. Classical examples of such events include the revolution and the experience of falling in love. We will never fall in love if we expect to fall in love. We will also not fall in love thinking that it is constantly possible that the right person could be just around the corner. We prepare for falling in love by becoming absolute fatalists who assume that the worst has always already happened and it is impossible to fall in love. It is no surprise, then, that Hegel was a fan of Diderot's *Jacques the Fatalist*. Assuming that everything is always already lost and the apocalypse has always already happened becomes the precondition for the emergence of a genuinely free act. Hegel's ends—of art, politics, philosophy (as science)—should be defended in these terms: they assume that there is no art and never will be; there is no politics and never will be; and there is no philosophy and never will be. There is nothing, less than nothing. This is Hegel's precondition for any real art, politics, or philosophy.

This conclusion may seem to make things worse, but in reality this is very good news because here Hegel defines for us the impossible yet necessary point from which true freedom emerges. Reason acts "as if, for it, all that preceded were lost and it had learned nothing from the experience of the earlier Spirits," but the "*inwardizing*, of that experience, has preserved it and is the inner being, and in fact the higher form of the substance." Assuming the apocalypse has always already taken place is thus not a simple negation of everything. Rather there is a torsion involved in this very act that entails the affirmation of an impossible point. Hegel calls this act a "release" (*Entlassen*).[54] The word *entlassen* has several connotations: (1) It means "to let something go"; for example, one releases a child into the world. (2) It means "to relieve something of its function" in the sense of discharging or dismissing, or even "to fire someone from a job." (3) It means that there is an act involved; this is what the *Ent* of *Entlassen* suggests. At the same time, however, the *lassen* implies that this act is an act of letting things be. This interpretation might bring it close to Heidegger's term *Gelassenheit*, but the two are not identical. We might even speak of *Entlassenheit*, although this is not an actual word. It is the very precondition of freedom, the very precondition of becoming a subject. *Entlassen* assumes that one becomes a free subject only if it happens that one does become a free subject. And this means that one can become a subject only when one sacrifices the very idea that one can or will ever become a subject. Hence one sacrifices both the very idea that one can become a subject and the illusion that there is anything in one's power or that one has any capacity whatsoever that could help.

The only way to prepare for becoming a subject (and this is what is at stake with absolute knowing) is to assume that God agrees with me, although he also admits that he does not exist, that everything is always already lost, that the apocalypse has always already happened, and that it is impossible but fully necessary to assume this knowledge. Only an absolute fatalist, a fatalist of the absolute, a fatalist of substance but also of the subject can be free. Žižek is therefore right in stating, "There is no contradiction between this 'fatalistic' aspect of Hegelian dialectics—the idea that we are simply taking note of what has already happened—and his claim to conceive substance as subject. Both really aim at the same conjunction, because the 'subject' is precisely a name for this 'empty gesture' which changes nothing at the level of positive content (at this level, everything has already happened) but must nevertheless be added for the 'content' itself to achieve its full effectivity."[55] In more precise terms, the fatalist gesture *is* the subject; it is the gesture of subjectivization. There is no subject without fatalism, and there is no fatalism without subjectivity. Subjects without fatalism are blind, and so is fatalism without subjectivity. This is why it may be no surprise that fatalism is so intimately linked to the history of rationalism, which has always been a theory of the subject. It took history until 1807, when the *Phenomenology of Spirit* was published, to reveal this, but this fact was not really a revelation.

The gesture of absolute fatalism is analogous to the image of a cartoon character running off a cliff, not noticing that it has no ground under its feet. The moment it looks down, it falls. Absolute fatalism, absolute knowing, or, in short, subjectivity is systematically located in the logical moment when the gaze turns down, sees the abyss, and starts to fall. This fall, *ein Fall*, is the very precondition to ever start running again, even if there still is no ground under one's feet. The fifth slogan of a provisory morality can thus take several forms: *Act as if the apocalypse had always already happened! Act as if everything were always already lost! Act as if you were dead!*

5
After the End

Freud against the Illusion of Psychical Freedom

*One spends three quarters of one's life wanting without doing . . .
and doing without wanting to.*
—Denis Diderot, *Jacques the Fatalist*

*There is far less freedom and arbitrariness in mental life, however,
than we are inclined to assume—there may even be none at all.*
—Sigmund Freud, "Delusions and Dreams in Jensen's *Gradiva*"

True hope has become with . . . Freud suspected of being an illusion.
—Jacob Taubes, "Religion und die Zukunft der Psychoanalyse"

How to Remain a Rationalist?

The unconscious does not know time. The same is true for
Freud, who somehow managed to make things worse after there
was not even nothing anymore, that is, after Hegel. From 1915 to
1917 Freud held the first series of his introductory lectures on
psychoanalysis that can be taken as a paradigm of how to make
things worst. After he first introduced his students to some of
the general issues one faces when attempting to study, teach, or
introduce psychoanalysis, he turned to the proverbial Freudian
phenomena of parapraxes, raising the question as to why that
which seems to be nothing but the "dregs . . . of the world of
phenomena" can legitimately play the role of a crucial object

for investigation and extensive study. He answers, "It is more promising in scientific work to attack whatever is immediately before one. . . . Since everything is related to everything, including small things to great, one may gain access even from such unpretentious work to a study of the great problems." Freud here unknowingly takes up Hegel's idea that any real science can start only by taking up what is before us, even if this is less than nothing. So, in this sense, Freud repeats Hegel. And he justifies his claim with an interesting argumentative move. He states that although trivial phenomena like a slip of the tongue and the misreading of a word may simply seem to be "small chance events" that deserve no deeper analysis, as soon as one assumes that there are "occurrences, however small, which drop out of the universal concatenation of events—occurrences which might just as well happen as not happen," this very assumption jeopardizes the very idea of rationalism. The reason for this is simple: if there are things that defy rational explanation, then rationalism is fundamentally limited in scope by those things that exceed rationality. Rationalism is thereby turned into a regional enterprise, and as soon as it loses the (allegedly impossible) possibility of totalizing its scope, it ultimately becomes meaningless. Again, the concept of totality is at stake here. If one presupposes that there are small or large events that defy rational explanation, one "has thrown overboard the whole *Weltanschauung* of science."[1] Rationalism cannot operate without (at least an attempt at) totalization that drives rationalism to inquire into the rationality even of that which appears irrational, or worse, arational. It is this seemingly trivial claim that marks one of the foundational gestures of psychoanalysis: the idea that *everything*, however minimal, however contingent it may appear, *deserves to be analyzed (and must be taken into account)*—a truly nonexclusive universalist stance. Freud therefore came up with the idea that the analyst's "evenly suspended attention" (*gleichschwebender Aufmerksamkeit*) corresponds to the analysand's "free association," to which I will return.[2] The idea behind the former is that *everything matters*. Everything is remarkable.

This means there is rationality even in alleged epiphenomena regardless of their nature. Methodologically speaking, rationalism needs "an evenly suspended attention," not shying away from taking excrescences or seemingly rubbish material as its object of inquiry.[3] Rationalism thus needs an *evenly suspended concept of reason*. Within this type of rationalism, rationality itself is an operational concept, which means that it is not substantially or a priori defined.[4] It operates instead in such a manner that it does not a priori exclude anything from its realm, even if this strategy may lead to surprising results. But if we presume, in contrast, the possibility of something happening without any determinable reason whatsoever, then we necessarily regionalize and substantialize reason and rationality. This position claims that some things happen for no reason at all, which implies that certain phenomena do not deserve an explanation because they are irrelevant for reason. (This is the substantializing move.) As a result certain phenomena also remain inexplicable, devoid of or even outside of reason. (This is the regionalizing move.) Although reason thinks it is entitled to be indifferent toward such phenomena, this very indifference embodies reason's weakness. The rationality that such proponents of reason defend is simply indifferent toward these phenomena because it does not have a proper explanation for them. Against the disavowed abolition of rationalism and reason, it helps, as Freud states, to recall "the *Weltanschauung* of religion," as even religion "behaves much more consistently, since it gives an explicit assurance that no sparrow fall from the roof without God's special will."[5]

Thus, according to Freud, true rationalism must begin with a peculiar inversion that takes place not only in the introduction to psychoanalysis but also at its very beginning. This inversion leads to the insight that previously ephemeral things akin to the sparrow falling from the roof (slips of the tongue and other parapraxes) are no longer irrelevant objects for rationalist and scientific investigation. And they may or, more precisely, *will* lead us to the core of human subjectivity.

Another consequence of taking these phenomena seriously is that these peculiar "objects" need to be taken into account in their material constitution (it is as if a Lutheran was reading the world). Considering this very constitution to be not merely ephemeral but crucial objects of and for reason, a rationalist has to perform a thorough *concrete analysis*, say of a concrete slip of the tongue. As Freud states, "We . . . enquire why it is that the slip occurred in this particular way and no other," which is why "we need only to take [the patient] at his word." Only in this way can we discover how the object was brought about as it was brought about. We always need to raise and answer the question of why a parapraxis, a dream, and so on "take[s] this particular form." The question is thus always, Why *this* (*dieses*)? This makes intelligible why already in the very beginning of Freud's introduction of and to psychoanalysis *rationalism and materialism coincide*. The stakes seem to rise immediately. We are concerned here not only with the defense and consistency of rationalism but also with the very existence of a peculiar kind of materialism that is able to take seriously every minimal concrete detail of the peculiar "object" of rationalism. But a materialist rationalism does entail another far-reaching twist: Freud's move not only inverts the hierarchy between the marginal and the central, the ephemeral and crucial phenomena, but also questions the hierarchical relation between what is considered to exist and that which is considered not to exist. As Freud states, this means that "even if dreams are superfluous . . .

they do exist" (a statement that also holds true for other alleg-edly irrelevant phenomena), as if modifying Charcot's famous line, "La théorie, c'est bon, mais ça n'empêche pas d'exister" ("The theory is all right, but it does not prevent something from existing nonetheless").[6]

Furthermore this move also emphasizes the fact that we can-not have an exclusive or substantialist concept of existence, which excludes something from legitimately existing. It also means that one must count as existing even that which bears no traits of existence. *We must be attentive to that which seems to inexist*: "One always needs to be attentive to that which inexists in the situation and not be content with what exists."[7] This is one of the crucial lessons linked to the very inversion that stands at the beginning of psychoanalysis. That which inexists in a given language may very well be that which is not-said, that which remains unsaid, which is why Lacan once stated, "We must be attentive to the unsaid that dwells in the holes in discourse, but the unsaid is not to be understood like knocking coming from the other side of the wall."[8] The unsaid—although it seems to not exist—is not located in some deeper layer behind or outside the doors of what is actually said. Rather it appears, or in-appears, in-exists (with the emphasis on both the prefix and the verb), in the midst, the tiny inconsistencies, the "holes" of what is said.

This is a crucial part of the fundamentals of *psychoanalytic materialist rationalism*. Such rationalism opposes the trivial idea of arbitrary happenings in psychical life and attacks the limita-tion of reason that follows from it. It sides with what appears to be superfluous or supernumerary rubbish and embraces it as a concrete material object for a concrete rational analysis, as an "object" of reason. Furthermore what follows from the inversion of the hierarchy between crucial and ephemeral "objects" for the study of the human psyche is a new idea of existence. Being attentive to what inexists or remains unsaid and concretely analyzing *this* peculiar inexistence, this singular unsaid "element," also implies being attentive to the cracks in what exists and appears and analyzing them in their very singular materiality. This clearly means that with this inversion of the classical hierarchy between existence and inexistence a different kind of materiality is brought into play, since these inexistent, unsaid objects do not exist as other objects of the world do (grandmothers, trees, birds, etc.). Freudian psychoanalysis thereby gives another very peculiar twist to the idea of materialist rationalism that it methodologically implies: the matter in question, the matter of the materialism at stake at the center of rationalism, is a different kind of matter, a matter that I am tempted to call (adding another term to the series of inexistence and unsaid) *un-matter* or immaterial matter. It should be clear that the *unconscious* is precisely the term that designates this very un-matter, this immaterial materiality that stands at the peculiar center of rationalism—the prefix *un-* indicating the "token of repression."[9] It does manifest itself in its effects (as Freud states, "It is true that the physician cannot learn of these unconscious processes until they have produced some effect on consciousness which can be communicated or observed" such that she can then "proceed by *inference*"), although these effects may not even exist in the ordinary sense of the term but rather in the form of ruptures, cuts, missing links, and so on.[10] The unconscious designates this peculiar un-matter or the immaterial materiality of that which does not exist, of that which remains unsaid, of the holes in discourse in which truth dwells. A rationalist needs to be attentive to this peculiar un-matter and avoid identifying it with mere arbitrariness, at least "if one wants to discover what is real in this world."[11] Psychoanalysis posits a different kind of Real that subverts the distinction of what exists and inexists, of what is and what is not.

Atta Choice! Countering the Presence of an Illusion

These fundamental inversions inscribed into psychoanalytic technique allow us to understand why Freud opposes what he refers to as "the illusion of there being such a thing as psychical freedom," an illusion that mankind usually does not want to give up.[12] By attacking the omnipresence of this illusion one thing becomes clear: what is at stake is a more profound choice between *psychical freedom and determinism*. Opting for psychical freedom abolishes rationalism's materialist mode of operation, sides with an exclusive concept of existence (and being), substantializes all concepts, and denies the reality of the unconscious. If we paint the picture in this way, it becomes clear that when dealing with the human psyche the choice between freedom and determinism can be only a choice for determinism. It follows the logic of the famous ultimatum "Your money or your life!" In this situation we have to choose giving away our money, as otherwise we would lose both our money and our life. In this sense the choice between freedom and determinism is predetermined and overdetermined by one of the two sides of the choice. At first it may appear surprising that the side of determinism predetermines a seemingly free choice. Yet if we perceive this choice to be a free choice, we have from the very beginning misperceived the nature of the choice. In other words, if we perceive this choice as a free choice, we have already fallen for the illusion of psychical freedom. We witness here an unsaid, at first glance hardly noticeable inversion: the choice cannot but be determined by the side of determinism, which proves to be a quite consistent and strong rational argument for determinism. Hence a true rationalist cannot but opt for psychical determinism, since she never had another choice. It is reason that does the choosing.

Speaking about a choice that is nothing but a forced choice may seem intuitively wrong. However, we cannot but opt for what seems wrong, namely the determinism that occurs in the determined character of the choice itself. One may wonder "how far one is prepared to go with Freud's insistence that the life of the mind contains no accident," yet what this question really asks is how far one is prepared to be a rationalist *and* a materialist.[13] This situation can, of course, provoke resistance. Freud's point, however, is that opting for what seems to be the wrong side enables something true to emerge. First, it allows us to see that the truth of this very choice resides on the side of determinism and with it a true materialist, rationalist standpoint. In short, without determinism no materialist rationalism can function in the sense delineated earlier. And thus without determinism, there can be no universalist perspective, in which "everything is related to everything."[14] Psychoanalytic rationalism hinges on the idea of a profound determinism, even in the last instance of the choice between freedom and determinism of psychical life. "To believe in determinism is to believe basically," Octave Mannoni rightly states, "that everything is subject to interpretation."[15] Determinism ensures the universalist dimension of rationalism and, with this, rationalism itself. This is why the "deeply rooted faith in undetermined psychical events and in free will . . . must yield to the demand of a determinism whose rule extends over mental life."[16]

It is important to note that Freud does not take this illusion to be a transcendental or transhistorical aspect of the human condition that would force mankind to believe in free will. On the contrary, he emphasizes that any faith in the indeterminacy and arbitrariness of psychical life (i.e., in free will), any form of "believing in chance," requires "a fair amount of intellectual education," since "primitive people and uneducated ones, and no doubt children as well, are able to assign a ground for everything that happens."[17] All of them also often share a peculiar "respect paid to dreams."[18] This point is instructive.

The illusion of psychical freedom emerges within culture and is therefore a constitutive cultural illusion—constituted by but also constitutive of culture. It makes it possible to avoid "admit[ting] to a sense of man's insignificance or impotence in the face of the universe."[19] Against such a disavowal of our helplessness, it is interesting to note that psychoanalysis seems to side with precisely those who have not (yet) properly entered culture and who do not (yet) share its illusion: the children, the uneducated, and the supposedly primitive peoples. Yet this does not imply that psychoanalysis is itself a regressive form of thought, aiming to return to some primordial precultural state. Rather psychoanalysis, as I argued earlier, is a fully and radically rationalist—and in this precise sense cultural—endeavor.

So how can we bring the highest peak of rationalism together with Freud's alliance with the uncultured? It is as if at the peak of culture the highest and the lowest coincide—another surprising dialectical inversion. Against the effects of cultural education that fend off all relation to the lower, earlier, or more primitive stages, Freud's psychoanalysis retrieves something from what seems to already have been left behind and overcome. At least with regard to free will, we can learn more from children and the uneducated, as there seems to be more reason in superstitions people actually have than in disavowed and obfuscated ones. The coincidence of the highest and the lowest that results from this radical form of rationalism makes it possible to contend that "our science is no illusion. But an illusion it would be to suppose that what science cannot give us we can get elsewhere."[20]

Psychoanalytic rationalism can demonstrate without any illusion that psychical life is fully determined and there is no such thing as psychical freedom. The illusion emerges precisely when we seek to avoid admitting that this fact renders us helpless. Therefore we displace the wish to be free onto something else, namely the culturally inculcated belief in free will. Thus at the core of cultural life rests an illusion diametrically opposed to what culture claims to be, namely rational. It is important to note that illusions are "not the same thing as an error" because, unlike errors, "they are derived from human wishes."[21] Human beings wish to be free, otherwise they would have to confront the fact that "obscure, unfeeling and unloving powers determine men's fate."[22] Wishing to avoid this fact leads to the creation of an illusion and may be one of the reasons culture functions at all. Culture functions by producing what Freud once called "a wishful reversal. Choice stands in the place of necessity, destiny. . . . A choice is made where in reality there is obedience to a compulsion."[23] The illusion of free will is a wishful reversal, something like the content of the primordial cultural repression. It results from the wish to avoid accepting that we are fundamentally determined. We do know it, but we do not want to believe what we know. The illusion generated by intellectual education and culture works as a defense mechanism against the efficacy of this very knowledge and with it against the core of what psychoanalysis teaches and what rationalism needs to defend. Here we can see why psychoanalysis cannot but be a theory of resistances against itself.

So psychoanalysis, as one of the highest cultural and rational techniques, intervenes against culture's own irrational product, against the illusory belief at the core of culture, in order "to deprive [man] of an instinctual satisfaction [*Triebbefriedigung*] and replace it by reasonable arguments [*Vernunftgründe*]."[24] It is thus fully rational and reasonable to give up the idea of free will and psychical freedom. Here a peculiar problem emerges: the illusion one believes in is itself not known to be an illusion; hence its proponents (i.e., believers) think of themselves as being fully rational agents, although they actually despise rationalism for the undeniable insights that result from it. It is as if a struggle within reason emerged, a struggle about what is rational, a struggle about what is reason within reason. We can think of ourselves as admirers of reason (this is what cultural education produces) and nonetheless assume the existence of free will (which is rationally untenable). This is why, in his attack on the illusion of freedom, *Freud defends reason even against its self-declared admirers*.

We need to draw consistent logical consequences from psychoanalysis's rationalism, however hard and disenchanting this might seem, but "no one, who has accepted the explanation of parapraxes can logically withhold his belief in all the rest."[25] If there is no psychical freedom and only determinism, what we have is psychical causality.[26] Being a rationalist means that psychical life can be accounted for in terms of determining psychical causes. This of course does not mean that psychical causality is identical to the natural causality that governs the world.[27] Here it is instructive to recall the precise point in Freud's lectures where he introduces the idea of psychical determinism against the illusion of free will. This distinction appears in a discussion of parapraxes, all the tiny deviations of everyday life, the mishaps that usually don't seem to warrant the interest of a scientist. But the claims of absolute psychical determinism and psychical causality must be related to precisely these phenomena. At the same time, "the unconscious is not the way that some inscrutable causality, beyond the apparent causality, always determines us, for the hidden unconscious causality beyond the apparent causality is not in itself constituted as a separate domain, it only emerges in the break of the apparent causality and cannot be grasped independently as something that would supplement and repair the crack. . . . But one can get to this only through the firm pursuit of determinism."[28] Freud's rationalist, materialist determinism is directly related to and necessarily leads to being attentive to those cracks, breaks, and ruptures within psychical causality, that without the determinist assumption we would not be able to perceive at all. In his lectures Freud himself refers his audience to his intensive study of these cracks and ruptures, the 1901 text *The Psychopathology of Everyday Life*.[29] In this earlier work Freud dealt with a whole range of parapraxes, such as forgetting (*Vergessen*), slips of the tongue (*Versprechen*), misreadings (*Verlesen*), slips of the pen (*Verschreiben*), and bungled actions (*Vergreifen*). But he also addressed the belief in chance, superstitious beliefs more generally, and so-called chance actions. To delineate Freud's determinism and its fatalist dimensions more clearly, it is thus necessary to return to this work and examine what has so far remained unsaid.

But before that, the series of *ver-* words enables a highly speculative remark. In a private conversation Mladen Dolar once drew a wonderful inference from the relevance of the prefix *ver-* in Freud's terminology that obviously includes all the terms just listed but also repression (*Verdrängung*) and negation (*Verneinung*). He raised the following question: What if the *ver-* not only indicates different forms of negation that one can typologize but also marks a peculiar type of negation at work in reason itself, in *Ver-nunft*. This raises the question, What would be *nunft*? Interestingly, etymologically *nunft* existed in Middle High German and was used in the sense of making use of an opportunity, taking a liberty, and even (juridically speaking) committing a rapacious theft. Could we then say that reason begins with a peculiar kind of opportunity? With a theft? With the taking and thus making of freedom?

Determinism in the Holes

In *The Psychopathology of Everyday Life*, Freud discusses a series of examples of forgetting of names: "It is no longer possible for me to take the forgetting of the name . . . as a chance event" because "one finds more and more frequently that the two

elements"—the forgotten name and that by which it is replaced—
"which are joined by an external association . . . possess in
addition some connection of content." There is an external
association that enables the mechanism of replacement. How
and by what a name is replaced is by no means an arbitrary event.
All depends on how we understand the external association
that determined the substitution of one name for the other.
This, Freud claims, also holds for chance actions, which "are
unobtrusive and their effects" are "slight." Even tics, like flip-
ping coins around in one's pocket or playing with one's hair,
reveal "something which the agent himself does not suspect in
them." These actions reveal something that, because of their
inconspicuousness, does not strike the agent of these actions.
He might not even consider himself fully responsible for them.
Although such actions seem to be innocent and meaningless,
they nonetheless present some meaning; although they seem to
be done for no reason at all, they are determined actions, caused
by something. Materialist rationalism thus holds that it is not
arbitrary that I play with my hair rather than my nose. Determinism's grasp is nonexclusively universal and firm. But what does
it mean to analyze what causes such actions? Freud's answer is
far from modest. It does not matter "in what detail these insignificant occurrences are determined by unconscious thoughts."
He who is able—by embracing utter psychic determinism—to
be "familiar with their significance may at times feel like King
Solomon who . . . understood the language of animals."[30]

Rational determinism allows us to deal with things that would
otherwise appear to be completely insignificant. It is as if one
were dealing with a language that otherwise would be inaccessible simply because it is a language different from all others and
thus might not even appear to be a language at all. In technical
terms, it is the language of symptoms. Freud, for example, calls
chance actions "symptomatic actions," and according to Lacan,

"the ego is structured like a symptom."[31] The precondition for understanding this language is not only the wholesale departure from belief in psychical freedom but also the departure from the idea of contingency itself. No human actions are contingent. All are determined in one way or another. This is why Freud claims that even finding money on the street is not a contingent event because it is fully determined by the "*unconscious* 'readiness to look for something.'" Even the concrete number one is thinking of is "strictly determined in a way that would really never have been thought possible." I am determined in a manner that I cannot but perceive as being impossible. Rationalism entails what appears to be an impossible determinism. It is impossible because, for example, "we believe that in general we are free to choose what words we shall use for clothing our thoughts or what images for disguising them," but "closer examination shows that other considerations determine our choice, and that behind the form in which the thought is expressed a glimpse may be had of a deeper meaning—often one that is not intended."[32] Whatever words we use, whatever things we do, there is some determination that comes to the fore even if it disappears again immediately. There is nothing in the human psyche that is not determined. Everything has a reason, and this is why there is no free will and no free choice. There is no way to escape this determination that affects all aspects of our lives. This total determination might appear to be impossible since one's own self-understanding suggests something else. Yet it is the affirmation of that which at first seems impossible that stands at the base of Freud's determinism.

In the last chapter of *Psychopathology*, Freud draws some general conclusions from his concrete investigations of numerous particular examples of the different forms of parapraxis. First, he restates that we need "to appreciate the extent of determination in mental life." But then he specifies this claim by contending that "many people . . . contest the assumption of complete psychical determinism by appealing to a special feeling of conviction that there is a free will. This feeling of conviction exists; and it does not give way before a belief in determinism. Like every normal feeling it must have something to warrant it." It is thus instructive to examine this feeling more closely. As Freud claims, it often happens "with regard to the unimportant, indifferent decisions that we would like to claim that we could just as well have acted otherwise: that we have acted of our free . . . will." When it does not matter what choice we make, we have the feeling that we experience the arbitrary freedom of the will (i.e., a kind of indifference). The same does not hold for "great and important decisions of the will," since then "the feeling that we have is rather one of psychical compulsion, and we are glad to invoke it in our behalf. ('Here I stand: I can do no other')." When something is at stake, we act like Luther did at Worms: we are and feel compelled. We feel free when nothing overly significant is at stake, and it is not even "necessary to dispute the right to the feeling of conviction" of freedom since it "informs us that conscious motivation does not extend to all our motor decisions." Even if one feels free, this very feeling tells us that free will does not extend to everything. So we just need to take it at its word, like a parapraxis itself. This feeling tells us that freedom is not at work when important things are at stake—say, falling in love or going mad. And it also tells us that freedom is not at work in little things either—say, biting one's fingernails. It seems that freedom itself admits that the biggest and the tiniest things are not part of its kingdom. And "if the distinction between conscious and unconscious motivation is taken into account," we can see that "what is thus left free by the one side receives its motivation from the other side, from the unconscious."[33]

Thus when I presume that I have the freedom to choose and

I choose arbitrarily, I leave it open as to why I chose option A and not option B. I attribute the sovereignty of choice to my free will and thus leave the reason for the choice undetermined. It is precisely in such a gap (of determination) that I end up being determined without willing it—and I even admit it (without willing to). This is why Freud can claim that "determination in the psychical sphere is still carried out without a gap," which indicates precisely the necessity for the totalizing reason that determinism allows for.[34] What resurges here is the choice between freedom and determinism as the structuring principle of all "choices" (even if they are perceived as free choices). Each choice we make, even concerning indifferent things, comes with the question of why we chose A over B (say, pizza over a hamburger). Freedom answers: Because of me, the freedom of decision. But this is not a real answer. This lack of an answer is where determinism enters. Free choice unwillingly abolishes itself precisely through this lack, this hole within the causality of free will, in the heart of freedom. Through this hole true determination comes to the fore. To be more precise, the true (unconscious) determination *is* this gap, *is* the unsaid, that which inexists in terms of free voluntary self-determination. Determination is that which exceeds the grasp of freedom and appears only as a hole or a gap in its causality. Yet it is this very gap that becomes the determining factor of free choice. This gap within the causality of freedom (Why this choice and not another?) reveals the true impact of psychical determinism. This is consistent with what Freud calls "the architectonic principle of the mental apparatus" that "lies in a stratification—a building up of superimposed agencies," namely the concept of superimposition.[35] The unconscious is not some agency that intervenes from beyond. It is there all the time, revealing itself in gaps, holes of what is actually willed, decided, said, and done. And, strangely enough, freedom itself admits to this fact and informs us of it. It points us to its gaps and limitations and thus to its being determined. There is a right to feel free but, even if we do so, we cannot but admit to what one assumed could not be admitted to.

After drawing this conclusion, Freud turns to a third and final remark: it is precisely this situation that shows us that conscious thought (and freedom) does not and cannot know of the motivation that appears in its gaps. Therefore "it would nevertheless be desirable to discover psychological proof of the existence of that motivation."[36] Where can we find such proof? One possible answer lies in psychoanalytic practice itself and its most fundamental principle: free association. After all, couldn't we say that, in the end, psychoanalysis does rely on a concept of freedom, namely the freedom of free association?

Einfall: Associate Freely Now!

In 1936 Freud wrote the following in a letter to Ernest Jones: "The replacement of hypnosis by free association took place before the *Interpretation of Dreams* between 1895 and 1900, at the same time I started to use the name of psychoanalysis."[37] Free association and psychoanalysis are thus co-emergent. This may be one of the reasons why free association is commonly referred to even by Freud as "the 'Fundamental Technical Rule,'" as the *Grundregel* of psychoanalytic practice.[38] As Lacan highlights, the law of free association also entails the law of non-omission, because of which everything is *remarkable*, and the law of non-systemization, because of which *everything* is remarkable.[39] The *Grundregel* stands at the ground of and determines psychoanalytic practice. Freedom and rule are not opposed but intertwined. So we should not assume that freedom lies at the fundament of psychoanalysis. To see why this is the case, we need to see how free association works.

Freud's most famous elaboration of free association can

be found in his 1913 essay "On Beginning the Treatment." He introduces free association after asking how an analysis is to be initiated and answers that this is a matter of indifference. What matters is that "the patient must be left to do the talking and must be free to choose at what point he shall begin."[40] Where to begin is indifferent and a matter of free choice, because the free will has a relation only to indifferent things. But this free point of departure relies on the logical coercion that one has to begin one way or the other and that there is no such thing as a neutral beginning. We are free under the condition that we begin somewhere—a forced freedom. If analysis is to begin, the fundamental rule, communicated in advance to the analysand, determines how it should work. The rule states:

> What you tell me must differ in one respect from an ordinary conversation. Ordinarily you rightly try to keep a connecting thread running through your remarks and you exclude any intrusive ideas that may occur to you and any side-issues, so as not to wander too far from the point. But in this case you must proceed differently. . . . You will be tempted to say to yourself that this or that is irrelevant here, or is quite unimportant, or nonsensical. . . . You must never give in to these criticisms, but must say it in spite of them—indeed, you must say it precisely *because* you feel an aversion to doing so.[41]

Analysis is not ordinary conversation; there is no need for consistency, no need to avoid nonsense or irrelevance. Everything must be said. This is why the fundamental rule also demands that there are no secrets. Feelings toward other persons and even their names must be expressed. Everything that comes to mind must be revealed at the moment that it comes to mind, even if it seems unimportant, nonsensical, or indecent. The fundamental rule forces the analysand to comply with it and to speak accordingly. If this works, what is thought and what is said become indistinguishable. This is no ordinary communication with explicit and implicit rules. Free association allows for isolating what is said (the signifiers) from the primacy and dominance of meaning. This is why psychoanalysis in this sense has nothing to do with hermeneutic interpretation. The elements that the analysand is reluctant to utter because they at first appear to be nonsensical later turn out to be significant. What in ordinary conversation might count as a mistake, say inconsistencies or contradictions, brings to the fore some truth about the speaking subject: "Truth grabs error by the scruff of the neck in the mistake."[42]

This is a peculiar freedom, in which you act as if you "were a traveler sitting next to the window of a railway carriage and describing to someone inside the carriage the changing views which you see outside."[43] The analysand is required to be an attentive and detached observer of the associative movement of his own thought, such that his speech mimetically repeats this associative movement. He looks at "the surface of his consciousness" and reports as honestly as possible.[44] He communicates everything that "comes to or 'falls into' mind (Einfälle), without selection, omission, evaluation, or concern for connection, sequence, propriety, or relevance."[45] Freud assumes that we can detect some sense in these in-falling things. When he literally speaks of Einfall, one should not too swiftly translate it as "idea." It also has the meaning of invasion (jemand fällt in etwas ein) and of collapsing (etwas fällt ein, like a building). In addition ein Fall is a case, and it is difficult to avoid thinking of "the fall" as original sin. Einfall is thus a speculative word in Hegel's sense of the term, since it unifies several contradictory meanings. If any Einfall should be communicated, how do we make sense of this peculiar concatenation of idea, invasion, and collapse?

Rebecca Comay convincingly argues that "the point of 'the free' association method is not to achieve freedom in any immediate or obvious way, and certainly not in the sense of autonomy, free will, or self-expression. It's about suspending the official rules of language but only so as to allow the real constraints to reveal themselves in their unembellished tyranny."[46] Along the same lines Freud himself asserted, "We must . . . bear in mind that free association is not really free." Why? Because the "patient remains under the influence of the analytic situation," and "we shall be justified in assuming that nothing will occur to him that has not some reference to that situation."[47] This means that the analysand is coerced and that there is a certain form of determination. The analyst demands, Associate freely when you speak to me! But "the freedom of 'saying no-matter-what' is suddenly transposed into its opposite; the opposite motion sets in the very moment one starts using this freedom, the predicament where the analysand would gladly say anything to cover this silence, but to no avail."[48] The fundamental rule of free association determines what is articulated. If freedom (of association) is the rule one has to obey, there is no (arbitrary) freedom (of free will). If one has to act, think, and speak freely, freedom itself turns out to be a determination that negates and abolishes free choice. The imperative to speak or act freely does not at all lead to freedom, no matter how much we want it to. Psychoanalysis makes us aware of this insight.

But free association cannot be simply a regulative idea for psychoanalytic practice. It must be there from the very start axiomatically. It implies that to some degree the analyst coerces the analysand. As Freud has it, "In a great many cases, with perseverance, an idea [*Einfall*] is extracted from the patient."[49] Through reiteration and repetition, free association brings to the fore what will have been there from the very beginning: the fundamental rule in its very practical effect(ivity) reveals that there always will have been a determination at the very beginning. It repeats, redoubles, and thereby brings to the fore the determinism at play in the subject's psyche. In this way the analyst once again creates the illusion of psychical freedom, but in such a way that it is at the same time, in the act of its creation, dismantled. Coercively creating the illusion of freedom (free association) enables one to reveal and demonstrate the function of real (disavowed and unconscious) determination. *Free association thereby exorcises an illusion by repeating the act of its constitution. In exorcising an illusion, it exorcises freedom.* Free association frees us from an illusion and allows us to relate differently to the determinism at the core of our being. What comes to light here is that a different concept of freedom is at stake in psychoanalysis—a freedom that is not in contradiction with determinism and is not a given capacity of my consciousness but something that emerges precisely when I am compelled and coerced.

What does this mean for the concept of *Einfall* and for the series of idea, invasion, and collapse? It means that through free association we first have the impression that ideas come to our minds freely and arbitrarily. This is again the materialist element of psychoanalytic rationalism. Determination reveals itself here. By means of the *Einfall*, we move in free association from having an idea to, second, the insight that an external force is at work within us that has invaded our mind and determined it. This impression of invasion collapses, third, the illusion of psychical freedom, as it completely demolishes the idea of free undetermined choice. In the practice of free association, we move from idea to invasion to collapse. All of this is part of an "education to truth against oneself."[50] One is freed from an illusion and led to truth, to an acceptance of one's own being determined. As Freud once stated without trying to be polemical, "Anyone who is to be really free and happy in love must have surmounted his respect for women and have come to terms with the idea of incest with his mother or sister."[51] Does this mean that we ultimately have to accept our psychical fate and destiny?

Driven Destiny Makes a Voice

In his works Freud frequently uses the terms *destiny* and *fate* (*Schicksal*). This is consistent with the idea that he formulated in 1906, that "what we call chance in the world outside can, as is well known, be resolved into laws. So, too, what we call arbitrariness in the mind rests upon laws, which we are only now beginning dimly to suspect. Let us, then, see what we find!"[52] So what did Freud find? What about fate and destiny? Most prominently, the concept of destiny—elided in the English translation—appears in the title of his 1915 "Instincts and Their Vicissitudes" ("Triebe und Triebschicksale"). Here Freud starts by introducing the *Grundbegriff*, the fundamental concept of the drive, as a constant force from which one cannot flee, as it compels us from the inside.[53] Its thrust lies in the sum of its force: it aims at satisfaction, its object is that by means of which it can reach its aim, and its source is basically unknown.[54] The concept of the drive is related to the problem of (psychical) determinism. In 1915 Freud believed that there were basically two kinds of drives, ego drives and sexual drives, which can come into conflict with one another. Against this background he enumerates four different modes of drive destinies that can emerge out of this conflict: (1) the aim of the sexual drives can be reversed and shift, say, from love to hate; (2) sexual drives can turn against the subject itself, as when sadism becomes masochism; (3) they can be repressed in order to avoid a conflict within the mind and the displeasure arising from it; and (4) they can be sublimated.

There are four ways of dealing with and determining what determines us: the drives, the four destinies of this determination. Freud calls these destinies "modes of *defence* against the instincts."[55] These defense operations work under the aegis of three fundamental polarities that for Freud govern the life of the mind: activity-passivity, ego-reality, and pleasure-displeasure. The four modes of destiny operate within these polarities. For example, love turns to being loved (from active to passive) when one attains a real relationship with someone and there lies more pleasure in being loved than in loving. The concept of destiny in this abstract rendering names first and foremost four possible defense formations against the drives that are determined by the three polarities. Its modes present what can happen to the drive(s). We should appreciate Freud's dialectical twist here: there are four modes of what to do with the drives, and there are many thinkable combinations. But the defenses do not abolish that which they defend against. Destiny is defensive, yet the drive as constant, coercive force can never be abolished. The drives might change for us (be inverted, turned, repressed, or sublimated), but in themselves they remain what they are.

This is why we can draw the conclusion that in a very precise sense the *drive is destiny* that manifests itself according to the four modes. As Žižek aptly remarks, "In this precise sense, one can claim that Freud's term *Triebschicksale*, the 'destinies/vicissitudes of drive,' is deeply justified, even tautological: the Freudian 'drive' *is* ultimately another name for 'Destiny,' for the reversal through which the circle of Destiny accomplishes/closes itself (when Destiny catches up with Oedipus, he is confronted with the fact that he is the monster he is looking for)."[56] Why is that? Because it is precisely that which seems external and alien to me (destiny) that determines the center of my being. I find within myself something that is not myself, but I am nonetheless responsible for it. Even worse, I have to acknowledge that what I take to be "myself" is not "myself" anymore. I am an unwelcome guest at a party that I initiated.

The drives that determine me and make me who I am are my

destiny, for which I am responsible. I am fully responsible for what I do with the drives because they are *fundamentally and continually* determining me. They not only fundamentally but also continually determine me because "repression does not hinder the representation of the drive from continuing to exist in the unconscious."[57]

Is it, then, an accident that psychoanalysis is closely linked to Oedipus, to "what is known as a tragedy of destiny"? At one point Freud himself raises the question of why the Oedipus story still moves us. He answers that this "can only be [because] its effect does not lie in the contrast between destiny and human will, but is to be looked for in the particular nature of the material on which that contrast is exemplified. There must be something which makes a voice within us, ready to recognize the compelling force of destiny in Oedipus, while we can dismiss . . . other modern tragedies of destiny. . . . His destiny moves us only because it might have been ours—because the oracle laid the same curse upon us before our birth as upon him."[58] Something creates a voice within us. And this something associates the story of Oedipus with our own. Something makes a voice; it speaks to us from within us, yet it is not simply ourselves speaking to ourselves. Rather it is as if we hear the voice of destiny itself within ourselves. We do not hear the oracle speaking but rather the drives making a voice. This is why Oedipus's fate might have been or will have been our own: not only because the Oedipus complex is "a structure universally bound to human destiny"—the curse that one first fancies Mommy and hates Daddy—but much more because it shows us that drives are destiny and that destiny emerges from our attempts to create defense formations against the drives, whereby we actualize precisely what we sought to prevent.[59] Oedipus's tragedy of destiny touches us because it depicts how it is attempting to avoid your own destiny that brings this destiny about. It shows us how our defense operation(s) against the drives determine the form in which our own fate is determined. We share with Oedipus that we are also "unwittingly bringing [our] fate on" ourselves.[60] Drive is fate, fate is driven, and psychoanalysis as rationalist theory of psychical determinism (i.e., of the drive and of the resistances against it) is ultimately a witty version of fatalism.

Anatomy Is Destiny I: The Fate of the Genitals

We cannot try to expound Freudian fatalism—and the notions of fate and destiny that it implies—without referring to the statement that incited endless criticism against Freud, the claim "Anatomy is destiny" ("Anatomie ist das Schicksal"). It was criticized frequently by feminists because Freud seems to endorse a form of biological determinism, which not only denies that "woman" and "man" are cultural, discursive constructions but also hierarchizes their relation (the infamous penis-envy thesis) and ultimately derives the inferior sociosymbolic positions of women from an unchangeable biological fact. If anatomy is destiny, anatomy forever determines who is superior or inferior.

Did Freud actually regress to a form of biological determinism? He used this formulation twice in his oeuvre, once in his 1912 essay "On the Universal Tendency to Debasement in the Sphere of Love Life," and once in the 1924 text "The Dissolution of the Oedipus Complex."[61] In both cases he claims to be modifying a saying of Napoleon's. When Napoleon met Goethe in Weimar in 1808, they discussed literature. They also talked about destiny plays (*Schicksalsstücke*), which Napoleon did not like. Napoleon then stated, "Politics is destiny."[62] Freud modifies this saying, adding the determinate article the (*das*) and replacing *politics* with *anatomy*: "Anatomy is the destiny."[63] Napoleon's claim suggests that destiny is made and the practice that brings it about is politics: "Policy occupies the place of ancient fate [La politique est la fatalité]."[64] Anatomy, on the other hand, does not seem practical at all but rather factual. So it is helpful to delineate the context in which Freud refers to this saying. In 1912 he uses this formulation after elaborating a far-reaching point concerning the relation between the subject and its sexual object. Their relation always seems problematic and is constitutively confronted with obstacles, whereas this is not the case with other relations in which someone likes something. (An alcoholic always has a good time as long as there are drinks.) Why is it different for sexual objects? Freud answers, "Something in the nature of the sexual drive itself is unfavourable to the realization of complete satisfaction."[65]

There are two reasons for this. First, any chosen sexual object of an adult (male) is already a surrogate for a sexual object that was prohibited by the barrier of incest (Mommy). This constitutive replacement creates an inconstancy within the object choice, for we cannot easily, and perhaps will never, find the perfect surrogate. Therefore we have to try over and over again. For the second reason, Freud turns to anatomy. The (more or less unified) sexual drive of the contemporary adult is formed in a long process of ontogenetic and phylogenetic cultural upbringing, a development not only of the subject but also of culture itself. In it certain components of the drive present in earlier stages come to be repressed: "These are above all the coprophilic instinctual components, which have proved incompatible with our aesthetic standards of culture, probably since, as a result of our adopting an erect gait, we raised our organ of smell from the ground. . . . But all such developmental processes affect only the upper layers of the complex structure." Freud here reiterates that the upper layers of complex defense formations may change, but "the fundamental processes . . . remain unaltered." And it is precisely here that anatomy enters the scene. For "the excremental is all too intimately and inseparably bound up with the sexual; the position of the genitals—*inter urinas et faeces*—remains the decisive and unchangeable factor. . . . 'Anatomy is the destiny.'"[66]

What does this mean? First of all, it means that there is no civilization without discontent. This is the high point of Freud's fatalism: the contingent fact that the genitals are located where they are "will make psychic conflict inevitable" because they become a reminder of what culture sought to do away with.[67] It is not that their position a priori determines our fate or inscribes a priori meaning into our destiny. Rather, through the progress of culture and the attempt to overcome previous stages of human organization, the utter meaninglessness of their location becomes somehow the metaphor of man's excremental nature (born between urine and feces) and the metonymy for human repression. The point is not that the anatomic fact as such determines our lives to be full of conflict. Rather it is precisely because there is culture that anatomy (the genital location) becomes fate. *Because of culture the anatomical placing of the genitals appears as a peculiar contradiction to culture.* Their location confronts us with what should have been done away with (like the uneducated, the primitive peoples, and the children with whom Freud aligned himself). It is as if culture seeks to depict human love life as noble. Yet the only way of believing this is to not think of the genitals while using them, since as soon as we think of them, we think of their location, and thus the noble thing literally turns to shit. This impasse is even greater, since the more we try not to think of the (location of the) genitals, the more we think of them. This makes one thing clear: (cultural) repression *is* the return of the repressed. Both coincide, and the place of this coincidence is the place of the genitals—a place that in itself is meaningless and contingent but that through the intervention of culture and repression is retroactively charged with embodying the return of all the shit one wanted to get rid of.

Freud's point is thus that it is only because there is culture and repression that this meaninglessness is associated with something that was supposed to be repressed and therefore determines our destiny. Culture generates the destiny of being confronted with conflicts that arise from the utterly meaningless place of our genitals. It is culture that makes anatomy into the destiny.[68] Culture, attempting to develop and to solve human problems, creates problems greater than those resolved—so great in fact that they can never be resolved, which produces the discontent that now seems inscribed into our nature. Things are thus not getting better, but they are not simply getting worse either. In fact with culture the worst has already happened. It is so bad that now the location of our genitals is what determines our destiny. One can see why Freud is a fatalist. Mankind's cultural achievement generates a meaningless fact that will have become a reminder of something that culture is unable to sublate. And, even worse, this meaningless reminder will as such have a determining impact on our fate. This means that with the emergence of culture, even our meaningless natural constitution will have been fundamentally out of joint—the universe is destabilized forever. One might translate the first meaning of "anatomy is the destiny" thus: The worst has happened, just look at our genitals!

Anatomy Is Destiny II: Male Illusions and Female Choices

Once again, "anatomy is the destiny"! In 1924 Freud uses this expression for the second time. And it is this use that brought him criticism from feminists. Again it is helpful to reconstruct the context in which this statement occurs. In "The Dissolution of the Oedipus Complex," Freud discusses different ways in which this complex can be overcome. Yet his main point does not concern the fact that it can be overcome but rather how it is done. He therefore focuses on the developmental stage that he calls phallic, in which the male child starts to use his genitals (masturbation), at the same time encountering the (parental) prohibitions against masturbation and against an incestuous object choice. Freud claims that this choice can be overcome if the prohibition is effectively linked to the threat of castration. The effect of the threat does not function through repression but as "a destruction and an abolition of the complex." This is why the true question for overcoming the Oedipal complex is, When does the threat of castration become effective? When does the child start to really believe in it? Freud answers: when the male child has observed a female genital, this "breaks down his unbelief."[69] Why? Because, from this moment on, the loss of his genitals becomes imaginable for the male child.

Female anatomy functions here as an authentication of prohibitive parental discourse. It provides the threat with a seemingly factual basis that there is someone who suffered the punishment due to violating the prohibition. Although Freud uses the expression only later in his text, we can still claim that the male child believes that the female *anatomy* represents *the destiny* of someone who violated the parental prohibition of incestuous Oedipal strivings.

But it is obvious that what the male child takes as proof is no proof at all. The male child believes that the castration threat ultimately means that he could become a woman, that is, a being who lost what it previously had as a result of being punished. But obviously, for Freud, a woman is not the result of actual castration. The male child believes he could be(come) a woman (lose "it") and thereby demonstrates his assumption that there are only men and castrated men (women). The result of this assumption is twofold: (1) Woman does not exist because all women are only castrated men. Man totalizes. (2) This perception of sexual difference that at the same time elides the real difference makes the threat of castration effective by being at the same time illusory in its very constitution. The abolition of the Oedipus complex originates in a constitutive illusion: (the means of) *overcoming Oedipus is an illusion.* So there is no way out of the illusion if the illusion is the way out. This is why it is a highly effective illusion and is productive of what Freud calls the superego. The threat of castration remains illusory and hence ineffective as long as there is no secondary illusion grounded in a misperception of female anatomy. It ascribes a meaning to female genitalia that they do not have and takes it as proof of what it does not prove. Only under the (clearly cultural) threat of castration does *female anatomy function as the destiny of man's own illusory misperception of his destiny.* Only by being duped does the male child leave the Oedipus complex behind. It treats the "structure universally bound to human destiny"—that is, Oedipus—as a structural and structuring illusion.[70] The misrecognition of anatomy is the key to this development.

After this elaboration Freud turns to the "far more obscure" development of the female child. It is more obscure as it does not follow the male logic of development. It is here that Freud uses the statement "Anatomy is the destiny" to emphasize that "the morphological distinction is bound to find expression in differences of psychical development."[71] Male and female children develop according to distinct logics. There is no parallelism, no relation, so to speak. We can see that Freud does *not* take the male perspective that sees in woman nothing but a castrated man, since then there would be no need for a second logic of development. He emphasizes the difference (which is what the male view does not do). If the male and the female child both love their mother, this situation is Oedipal only for the male child. The male child is directly born into the Oedipus complex, and he overcomes it by the illusion that the threat of castration effectuates. The female child moves from (what the male child sees as) the reality of castration, that is, from the castration complex to the Oedipus complex, and in this move she even has to shift the sex of the libidinal object (from mother to father), which the male child does not have to do. There is thus a strictly inverted logic. The one moves from having "some thing" to being afraid of losing it, the other from lacking "it" to . . . ? Freud enumerates three developmental destinies for the female child: (1) The female child believes that she is a kind of crippled man that may be able to become a real man (someday). This is clearly also an illusion that actually mirrors, quite literally, the male development and shares the male gaze on femininity. It also assumes there are only men and deficient or castrated men (penis envy). (2) The female child turns away from sexuality and seeks to neutralize it. She seeks to be neither male nor female. In one way or the other this is a version of discursive constructivism and implies the repression (with all its deadlocks) of sexual difference. (3) The female child embraces her condition and accepts that she is castrated from the very beginning. This also enables her to enter the Oedipal setting after a complicated development. These three options are how to deal with female anatomy. Anatomy thus generates only one destiny for the male, but three destinies for the female.

The three options are theoretically distinguishable, although in real life they are often mixed. But as Freud also claims that all human beings have a "bisexual disposition and cross-inheritance" so that they combine "in themselves both masculine and feminine characteristics," he does not assign the female and the male logic only to either the male or the female biological gender once and for all. Here things are getting even more complex.[72] In any case it is clear that only the third option of the female logic makes the girl into a woman. If the male logic moves from a universally binding structure to the reign of a structural illusion, we can see that with the three female destinies something else emerges: the insight that there is a peculiar forced choice. One cannot not chose which subject one will be, and this choice determines the way one will fantasize, dream, desire, and enjoy. This holds for both biologically male and biologically female subjects, yet it can be thought of only from the side of female logic. What does this mean? One way of answering this question is to recall the trivial yet often forgotten insight that in relation to our own dreams we do not have the impression of having freely fabricated them. For this reason we might be tempted not to feel responsible for them (even more so if one dreams of something that one thinks is nasty). Yet who else but ourselves could be responsible for our own dreams? The choice involved in the female logic of subjectivization is located on the same plane. This peculiar kind of choice to which we are condemned is structurally analogous to what Freud calls "'the choice of neurosis'"—a choice that is peculiarly "independent of experiences."[73] This means that in a certain sense the subject is forced to choose its own unconscious: "This claim that the subject, so to speak, chooses her unconscious . . . is the very condition of possibility of psychoanalysis."[74] This is directly related to the concept of psychical causality that I referred to earlier. In the beginning there is a crack—the beginning is an Ur-Sprung—which appears in the form of a forced choice. This choice is our fate. This point is directly related to the expression "Anatomy is the destiny." Only by emphasizing the difference between the two logics, that is, by emphasizing sexual difference, through the deviation from the male logic (i.e., the woman), does a kind of freedom appear that is neither arbitrary nor simply conscious (and related, say, to an object in the world). This choice constitutes our own unconscious predispositions (the way we dream, etc.) and cannot not be made. It is not a free choice but the embodiment of a different kind of freedom.

In some sense this also means that only the deviation from the male logic, that is, the female logic, allows us to see the utter meaninglessness of anatomic dispositions for what they are: the (return of the) repressed of culture. It thereby allows us to take a different approach to the fundamental structuring principle of human life, the Oedipus complex. That woman chooses to enter the Oedipal structure (third destiny) *is* precisely the equivalent of choosing one's own unconscious. By comprehending this peculiar choice as a choice, we can see that even Oedipal desire is not primordial; it is preceded by a choice. The female is in this precise sense always pre-Oedipal and will therefore always already be post-Oedipal. This structure also suspends the threat of castration. Linking Freud's two claims together, the claim "Anatomy is the destiny" means that our fate is to assume that with the onset of culture the worst has already happened. It means that there is sexual difference (male and female anatomy and logic), and it means that only the (logically) female is able to embrace both at the same time: saying that the worst has already happened goes hand in hand with saying that sexual difference has already happened. Only the female logic allows us to act as if we had nothing to lose. Courage is female. Only this logic allows for a break with the facticity of threats (including the threat of castration), for a rupture with structure (Oedipus) and with totalizing male logic. It allows us to see that "man is not only much more unfree than he believes"—as everyone is forced to choose his unconscious—"but also much freer than he knows" (as there is always the choice of how to dream, desire, etc.).[75] The fact that it is the female logic that makes all this visible means that, for Freud, *woman* is the name of this peculiar freedom that we know nothing of. But if *woman* is a name for this choice, this also means that within the female logic woman does not exist (as a fixed entity). Rather *woman* is a name for this act. Freud's fatalism implies that we should give up all illusions of psychical freedom and embrace the idea that we are condemned to determine the way we are (unconsciously) determined. In this fatalism "Anatomy is destiny" becomes an emancipatory slogan. We can derive from this the sixth slogan of a contemporary provisional moral: *Act as if you were an inexistent woman!*

Last Words

*I see nothing. It's because there is nothing, or it's because I have
no eyes, or both, that makes three possibilities to choose from.*
—Samuel Beckett, *The Unnameable*

*Tragedy is when I cut my finger. Comedy is when
you fall down an open sewer and die.*
—Mel Brooks

Start by expecting the worst! Act as if you did not exist! Act as if
you were not free! Act in such a way that you accept the struggle
you cannot flee from! Act in such a way that you never forget to
imagine the end of all things! Act as if the apocalypse has always
already happened! Act as if everything were always already lost!
Act as if you were dead! Act as if you were an inexistent woman!
These are the astounding slogans of a contemporary provisional morality that can be derived from the history of Western
rationalist thought. These are slogans of fatalism, derived from
Luther, Descartes, Kant, Schmid, Hegel, and Freud. Just enu-
merating them produces a strange, comic effect. In fact they
may all sound a bit ridiculous. Yet it is precisely their apparent
ridiculousness that puts them at the center of the rationalist
fatalism for which I made a plea—a fatalism that is necessarily
comic and that I therefore want to call *comic fatalism.*

In Brecht's brief, charming piece "Hegelian Dialectic," which consists of a dialogue between two characters, Ziffel and Kalle, the former makes an ironic plea for Hegel as the "greatest humorist among the philosophers." He classifies the *Science of Logic*—crucial cornerstone of Hegel's entire system—as "one of the greatest humoristic works of world literature" because it is about the "custom of the concepts, these slippery, unstable, irresponsible existences." Ziffel argues that it is about "how they fight each other . . . and . . . enter so to say in pairs, each is married to its opposite. . . . They can live neither with nor without each other."[1] It is precisely such humor, which Lacan once attributed to Hegel, that is a crucial element of fatalism.[2]

The coincidence of opposites, freedom born from fatalism, fatalism as precondition of freedom. Why is this comic? Before returning to Hegel, we may start with a nonphilosophical experiment. Open your computer's browser and search for fatalism. Then look at the images that you have found. They will be mostly funny pictures. This may be either because we cannot take fatalism seriously or simply because fatalism has an inherently comic nature. The reason for this might lie in the recoiling and inverting moves of fatalism: we need to defend divine predestination just to get rid of God in a proper manner, so that God himself admits that he does not exist, as Hegel demonstrates. We need to shift our gaze a bit to see that we should have always already been falling into the abyss, since we were walking on thin air rather than on solid ground, as all the thinkers of fatalism argue. This also means that the apocalypse that fatalism assumes is finally a comic concept. As fatalists, we do not have to fear the worst or at least hope for something else, but we must assume that it has always already taken place. Only by affirming this assumption can we become emancipated from the highly problematic stance on freedom that articulates it as possibility and capacity. We thus have to assume the necessity of the impossible. But it is important to point out that the fatalism at stake here is not simply ridiculous but comic—and only by being comic can it provide a precondition of freedom. This is a fatalism without fate, since everything has always already taken place.

But, again, why should this be comic? Alenka Zupančič has rightly contended that "there is little doubt that among classical philosophers, Hegel was the one who valued comedy and the comic spirit most highly."[3] Already in 1802–3 he stated, "Tragedy arises when ethical nature cuts its inorganic nature off from itself as fate—in order not to become embroiled in it—and treats it as an opposite; and by acknowledging this fate in the ensuing struggle, it is reconciled with the divine being as the unity of both. Comedy, on the other hand (to develop this image further) will generally come down on the side of fatelessness." Tragedy is structured around and presents a struggle with fate—a fate that is brought about precisely by the ethical agent who seeks to get rid of it. Yet this ethical agent is ultimately reunited with substance (the divine being) since it ultimately has to recognize that from which it started to free itself. Comedy, in contrast, presents the absence of fate. In doing so it falls either "under the heading of absolute vitality, and consequently presents only shadows of antagonism or mock battles with an invented fate and fictitious enemy [or] under the heading of non-vitality and consequently presents only shadows of independence and absoluteness. The former is the old (or Divine) comedy, the latter is the modern comedy."[4] This last point is intricate. Ancient comedy presents an absolute vitality that is driven by fake battles and struggles with fictitious enemies, whereas modern comedy presents nonvitality that is stuck precisely because of shadows of independence and absoluteness.

How to make sense of all this against the background of our present investigation? Here it is instructive to return briefly to Hegel's discussion of ancient and modern comedy in his *Lectures on the Fine Arts*. In comedy, Hegel states, even though "characters dissolve everything, including themselves, the victory of their own subjective personality . . . nevertheless persists self-assured."[5] Zupančič has elaborated this structure by referring to the archetypal scene in which, for example, an arrogant aristocrat slips on a banana peel. What makes such a scene comic? It is comic, she argues, not because in the moment of the fall we see that he who believes himself to be better is reminded by reality that he too is only a limited, finite human being. Rather what makes such a scene comic "and makes us laugh most in our archetypal (imaginary) comedy is not simply that the baron falls into the puddle but, much more, that he rises from it and goes about his business as if nothing has happened."[6] The structure of comedy overall lies in this gesture of continuing even after everything seems to have been relinquished, including the character himself.

Hegel elaborates the general structure of comedy by pointing out that ancient comedy presents this logic only within its content, whereas modern comedy includes it in the very form of comedy itself. In ancient comedy we laugh when we see that "the realization of an end is at the same time the end's own destruction."[7] Kant had already claimed that we laugh when "a tense expectation is transformed into nothing," and we should emphasize here the Nothing that makes us laugh.[8] Hegel's point is quite similar: when the realization of an end coincides with its own relinquishment and destruction, there appears a peculiar Nothing that makes us laugh. Therefore we are not only dealing with an act of self-negation (of ends by means of their realization), but it is precisely this self-negating act that produces something, that is not something, that makes us laugh. It is important that this self-negation is comic because in comedy there is "confidence felt by someone raised altogether above his own inner contradiction and not bitter or miserable in it at all; this is the bliss and ease of a man who, being sure of himself, can bear the frustration of his aims and achievements." In comedy there is no bitter conflict because in the very frustration of one's aims and achievements, there is an achievement of a different kind. Comedy demonstrates that if nothing is achieved, it is precisely Nothing that is achieved—and although this may sound comical, it is quite hard to achieve (maybe just because it is somehow always already there). This conclusion is not at all simply grotesque or satiric because comedy functions by bringing "the absolutely rational into appearance."[9] Demonstrating how Nothing is achieved, comedy presents the appearance of the absolutely rational. We can already see in which sense the fatalism I defend has a necessary comic dimension.

Modern comedy, for Hegel, takes up this dimension of ancient comedy and makes it into the very determining factor of its form. Thus if ancient comedy still functioned within an objectively given setting in which the self-negating acts of the characters are presented, modern comedies eliminate even this remainder of objectivity. The problem is no longer only that the comic characters pursue ends or aims that in their very realization prove their nullity by self-destructing. Modern comedies do also not entail any "necessary development." This means that now "the dramatis personae are comical themselves"—like the aristocrat falling into the puddle.[10] The characters themselves become comical and not only the ends of their actions or their attempts to pursue these ends in the setting or situation in which they appear. The comic thus appears to be inscribed into the very kernel of subjectivity. Therefore modern comedies depict not only the necessity of contingency (as there is no necessary development of any character whatsoever) but also the contingency of necessity: they show how characters stick to some orientation for contingent reasons—something that thereby becomes their *unary trait* (say, being a miser)—that, precisely because they stick to it for contingent reasons, demonstrates the contingency of necessity.[11] Modern comedy thereby eliminates every objective ground, even the last grain of givenness, by emphasizing the necessity of contingency and the contingency of necessity at the ground of subjectivity. What is achieved thereby is no longer nothing, as in ancient comedy, but even less: less than nothing, a nothing that is deprived even of its substance, of its nothingness. We can thus see why the fatalism defended here cannot but be comic: Nothing, less than Nothing . . . Fatalism, the pure comic fatalism.

Emphasizing that fatalism needs to be comic also allows us to distinguish it from three other versions of fatalism: the tragic, the existentialist, and the nihilist. *Tragic fatalism* claims that tragic conflict is unavoidable, that it is even mostly unavoidably produced in the very attempt of avoiding it, and that the (social and political) human condition therefore entails a conflict that one cannot but try to resolve, which thereby, first of all, constitutes the conflict as conflict. Comic fatalism, however, asserts against tragic fatalism that only one thing is unavoidable: we cannot avoid the insight that everything is always already lost and that our endeavors to do so are actually comic. We cannot avoid embracing the fact that there is less than nothing to embrace. There is therefore no human condition and no conflict. There is not even any true history or true life. How could there be any human condition properly speaking? *Existentialist fatalism* also emphasizes the human condition but ultimately asserts that freedom relies on freeing oneself from all external determination just to discover the nothingness inside of oneself—the nothingness that is freedom and the only thing we can rely on. Comic fatalism asserts against existentialist fatalism that there is not even a stable or given nothing or nothingness to rely on. *Nihilistic fatalism*, finally, emphasizes the nullity of everything and devalues all that is. Comic fatalism asserts against nihilistic fatalism that there is nothing to be devalued and that devaluation therefore is in itself a null gesture. Comic fatalism is close to what Nietzsche once coined "active nihilism," which, he says, is the form of "the highest fatalism, but identical with *chance* and the creative."[12] Comic fatalism therefore relates to nihilistic fatalism as active nihilism relates to passive nihilism in Nietzsche. Comic fatalism recoils back upon itself and thus turns the apocalypse into a category of comedy.

If a comic—and overexaggerated—fatalism is the outcome of the history of philosophy, comedy is rationalist, and comic fatalism is a reasonable position to defend. Its comic element, as Zupančič has shown, is precisely its subjective element. It is the logical moment when the gaze of the cartoon figure turns down into the abyss and it realizes that it simply ignored what it knows—namely that we need to fall when walking off the edge of a cliff. This book is an attempt to turn the gaze, if ever so slightly.

Comic fatalism follows one ultimate—paradoxically foundational—rule, and the paradoxical structure of this rule is also what makes it comic. This rule is that *there is no there is*. This is a properly Hegelian speculative proposition. But the comic element does reside not solely in the rule itself but also in the place of its articulation because it is self-annulling. The very form of this rule bears the mark of modern comedy, as depicted by Hegel. It therefore comes close to the Cretan liar's paradox (the liar's statement that he is lying). But the liar is more concerned with the truth content of a seemingly self-contradictory statement when uttered from a position that seems to contradict the very content of the statement. "There is no there is," in contrast, is an impossible proposition that nonetheless can be stated without simply turning into nonsense. "There is no there is" assumes a position of articulation that the proposition itself consequently invalidates. One is within the movement of this proposition thrown back to its very beginning that will have been altered due to this very move. After reaching the predicate, we are thrown back to the very place of its articulation, which will have become different, always already lost within the movement of the proposition itself. Comic fatalism affirms such an impossible position of articulation as both absolutely necessary and impossible. Only such a gesture liberates us from all givenness, from all possibilities of realizing a given capacity. Only such a gesture can provide a precondition for thinking and enacting freedom.

So how can we prepare for the real movement that abolishes the present, the given state of things (I assume the reader is able to decipher this reference)? One first step is to defend the idea that freedom can exist only if there is no there is. But who is the one saying this, if there is no philosophy and never will be?

NOTES

INTRODUCTION

Denis Diderot, *Jacques the Fatalist and His Master* (London: Penguin, 1986), 98.

1. Karl Marx, *Capital Volume 1*, in Karl Marx and Friedrich Engels, *Collected Works*, vol. 35 (London: Lawrence & Wishart, 1987), 186.

2. For an analysis of this logic, see Mladen Dolar, "Officers, Maids, and Chimney Sweepers," unpublished manuscript, 2014; Slavoj Žižek, "The Role of Chimney Sweepers in Sexual Identity," *International Journal of Žižek Studies* 7, no. 2 (2013): 1–9.

3. Karl Marx and Friedrich Engels, *The Communist Manifesto* (London: Pluto, 2008), 56.

4. For a detailed discussion of the intricacies and deadlocks involved in the freedom of choice, see Renata Salecl, *The Tyranny of Choice* (London: Profile, 2011).

5. Frank Ruda, "How to Act As If One Were Not Free? A Contemporary Defense of Fatalism," *Crisis and Critique* 1, no. 3 (2014): 175–99.

6. Leszek Kolakowski, *God Owes Us Nothing: A Brief Remark on Pascal's Religion and on the Spirit of Jansenism* (Chicago: University of Chicago Press, 1998), 190; Alain Badiou, *Metapolitics* (London: Verso, 2012).

7. Glaucon at one point of the debate on the "luxurious city" states that it will be "a city of pigs." Plato, *Republic* (Cambridge MA: Hackett, 2004), 51.

8. Gilles Châtelet, *To Live and Think Like Pigs: The Incitement of Envy and Boredom in Market Democracies*, (Falmouth, UK: Sequence, 2014).

9. A detailed reconstruction of Buridan's ass can be found in Nicolas Rescher, *Scholastic Meditations* (Washington DC: Catholic University of America Press, 2005), 1–48. See also Justin Clemens, "Spinoza's Ass," in *Spinoza Now*, ed. Dimitris Vardoulakis (Minneapolis: University of Minnesota Press, 2011), 65–98.

10. Marquis de Sade, *Florville and Courval, or Fatality*, in *The Crimes of Love: Heroic and Tragic Tales* (Oxford: Oxford University Press, 2005), 98–142.

11. I borrow this term from Stanley Cavell, *Pursuits of Happiness: The Hollywood Comedies of Remarriage* (Cambridge MA: Harvard University Press, 1984).

12. Pierre Klossowski, "A Destructive Philosophy," *Yale French Studies* 35 (1965): 61–80.

13. Rebecca Comay, "Adorno avec Sade," *differences* 17, no. 1 (2006): 15.

14. Comay, "Adorno avec Sade," 17.

15. Kolakowski, *God Owes Us Nothing*, 76.

16. Slavoj Žižek, "Only a Suffering God Can Save Us," in Slavoj Žižek and Boris Gunjevic, *God in Pain: Inversions of the Apocalypse* (New York: Seven Stories, 2012), 162.

17. Klossowski, "A Destructive Philosophy," 69.

18. Sophocles, *The Oedipus Coloneus*, in *Sophocles: The Plays and Fragments* (Cambridge, UK: Cambridge University Press, 2010), 193.

19. Kathy Acker, "Reading the Lack of the Body: The Writing of Marquis de Sade," in *Must We Burn Sade?*, ed. Deepak Narang Sawhney (New York: Humanity, 1999), 241.

20. Jean-Pierre Dupuy, *Pour une catastrophisme éclairé: Quand l'imposible est certain* (Paris: Seuil, 2002); Jean-Pierre Dupuy, *Economy and Faith: A Crisis of Faith* (East Lansing: Michigan State University Press, 2014).

21. Žižek, "Only a Suffering God Can Save Us," 162.

22. Michel Foucault, "Lives of Infamous Men," in *Essential Works of Foucault, 1954–1984*, vol. 3 (New York: New Press, 2001), 157–75.

23. G. W. F. Hegel, *The Science of Logic* (New York: Humanity, 1969), 836. See also Slavoj Žižek, *The Ticklish Subject: The Absent Center of Political Ontology* (New York: Verso, 2000), 79.

24. Hegel, *Science of Logic*, 836.

25. G. W. F. Hegel, *Phenomenology of Spirit*, trans. A. V. Miller (Oxford: Oxford University Press, 1977), 37.

26. Hegel, *Phenomenology of Spirit*, 37.

27. René Descartes, *Discourse on Method*, in *The Philosophical Writings of Descartes*, vol. 1 (Cambridge, UK: Cambridge University Press, 1985), 122.

28. Alain Badiou, "Le courage du present," *Le Monde*, February 13, 2010, http://www.lemonde.fr/idees/article/2010/02/13/le-courage-du -present-par-alain-badiou_1305322_3232.html.

1. PROTESTANT FATALISM

Denis Diderot, *Jacques the Fatalist and His Master* (London: Penguin, 1986), 56; Jean-Paul Sartre, *The Words* (New York: Braziller, 1981), 250; Every Time I Die, "Decaying with the Boys."

1. Richard Marius, *Martin Luther: The Christian between God and Death* (Cambridge MA: Harvard University Press, 2000), 467. The present chapter owes a lot to one of the most impressive contemporary readers of the Reformation tradition: Felix Ensslin.

2. Ernstpeter Maurer, *Luther* (Freiburg: Herder, 1999), 49.

3. For this, see: Alain Badiou, *Saint Paul: The Foundation of Universalism* (Stanford: Stanford University Press 2003).

4. Maurer, *Luther*, 49.

5. Martin Luther, *Disputation against Scholastic Theology*, in *Luther's Work*, vol. 31: *Career of the Reformer 1* (Minneapolis: Fortress, 1957), 12.

6. Maurer, *Luther*, 51.

7. Franz Rosenzweig, "Scripture and Luther," in Martin Buber and Franz Rosenzweig, *Scripture and Translation* (Bloomington: Indiana University Press, 1994), 58.

8. E. Gordon Rupp and Philip S. Watson, eds., *Luther and Erasmus: Free Will and Salvation* (Louisville KY: Westminster, 1996), 37, 38, 40.

9. Rupp and Watson, *Luther and Erasmus*, 47, 48, 49.

10. Rupp and Watson, *Luther and Erasmus*, 49, 50.

11. Rupp and Watson, *Luther and Erasmus*, 15, 53.

12. Rupp and Watson, *Luther and Erasmus*, 77, 89, 71.

13. Rupp and Watson, *Luther and Erasmus*, 79, 85.

14. Rupp and Watson, *Luther and Erasmus*, 85, 97.

15. Rupp and Watson, *Luther and Erasmus*, 89, 92, 93, 94, 95, 97.

16. Lee Gatiss, "The Manifesto of Reformation: Luther vs. Erasmus on Free Will," *Churchman* 123, no. 3 (2009): 215, 208.

17. Rupp and Watson, *Luther and Erasmus*, 236. See also Felix Ensslin, *Die Entbehrung des Absoluten: Luther mit Lacan*, unpublished manuscript, 2009.

18. Theodor W. Adorno, *Minima Moralia: Reflections on a Damaged Life*, trans. E. F. N. Jephcott (New York: Verso, 2005), 49.

19. Alexander Garcia Düttmann, *Philosophy of Exaggeration* (London: Continuum, 2007).

20. Rupp and Watson, *Luther and Erasmus*, 291–92.

21. Benjamin B. Warfield, "The Theology of Reformation," in *Studies in Theology: The Works of Benjamin B. Warfield*, vol. 9 (Grand Rapids MI: Baker, 2003), 471; Roland H. Bainton, *Here I Stand: A Life of Martin Luther* (Nashville TN: Abingdon, 1978), 93–94.

22. Cf. R. C. Sproul, *Willing to Believe: The Controversy over Free Will* (Grand Rapids MI: Baker, 1997), 100.

23. Rupp and Watson, *Luther and Erasmus*, 326, 303, 221, 223, 248, 125, 126, 224.

24. Gatiss, "The Manifesto of Reformation," 100; Rupp and Watson, *Luther and Erasmus*, 125.

25. Rupp and Watson, *Luther and Erasmus*, 127, 128, 130.

26. Rupp and Watson, *Luther and Erasmus*, 129, 130, 134.

27. See Heiko Oberman, *The Dawn of Reformation: Essays in Late Medieval and Early Reformation Thought* (Grand Rapids MI: T&T Clark, 1986).

28. Rupp and Watson, *Luther and Erasmus*, 136.

29. Rupp and Watson, *Luther and Erasmus*, 136, 137, 244.

30. See Maurer, *Luther*, 123.

31. Rupp and Watson, *Luther and Erasmus*, 234.

32. Sproul, *Willing to Believe*, 100.

33. Slavoj Žižek, *The Ticklish Subject: The Absent Centre of Political Ontology* (London: Verso, 2009), 18.

34. Reiner Schürmann, *Broken Hegemonies (Bloomington: Indiana University Press, 2003)*, 374.

35. Rupp and Watson, *Luther and Erasmus*, 138.
36. Rupp and Watson, *Luther and Erasmus*, 139, 266, 297, 305, 299, 234, 232, 243, 258.
37. Rupp and Watson, *Luther and Erasmus*, 219, 278, 290, 141, 170, 175, 292, 180, 254, 159, 167.
38. Rupp and Watson, *Luther and Erasmus*, 308, 328, 178, 174, 179.
39. Rupp and Watson, *Luther and Erasmus*, 312, 236, 212, 252, 185, 190.
40. Rupp and Watson, *Luther and Erasmus*, 201.
41. Rupp and Watson, *Luther and Erasmus*, 200.
42. Ensslin, *Die Entbehrung des Absoluten*.
43. Max Weber, *The Protestant Ethic and the Spirit of Capitalism* (London: Routledge, 1992), 62. In contrast, see Herman Westerink, *The Heart of Man's Destiny: Lacanian Psychoanalysis and Early Reformation Thought* (London: Routledge, 2012).
44. Rupp and Watson, *Luther and Erasmus*, 229, 207, 225, 263.
45. Rupp and Watson, *Luther and Erasmus*, 209, 232, 200, 214, 207, 212, 231.
46. Rupp and Watson, *Luther and Erasmus*, 244, 280.
47. Rupp and Watson, *Luther and Erasmus*, 259, 265, 245, 286, 288.
48. Rupp and Watson, *Luther and Erasmus*, 289, 211, 217, 320, 307, 314, 289.
49. Rupp and Watson, *Luther and Erasmus*, 329.
50. Maurer, *Luther*, 35.

2. RENÉ THE FATALIST

Denis Diderot, *Jacques the Fatalist and His Master* (London: Penguin, 1986), 142; René Descartes, "Letter to Mersenne (9 January 1639)," in *The Philosophical Writings of René Descartes*, vol. 3: *The Correspondences*, trans. John Cottingham et al. (New York: Cambridge University Press 1991), 131; Stéphane Mallarmé, "Notes sur le langage (1869)," in *Oeuvres complètes*, vol. 1 (Paris: Pléiade, 1998), 205; Alain Badiou, "Event and Truth: Part 4," November 30, 2013, https://www.youtube.com/watch?v=AWYZUczVpss.
1. G. W. F. Hegel, Lectures on the History of Philosophy, vol. 3: Medieval and Modern Philosophy (Lincoln: University of Nebraska Press, 1995), 224; Edmund Husserl, Cartesian Meditations: An Introduction to Phenomenology (Dordrecht: Kluwer, 1977), 4.

2. René Descartes, The Passions of the Soul, in The Philosophical Writings of René Descartes, vol. 1 (New York: Cambridge University Press, 1985), 339.

3. A more challenging reading of the pineal gland and its systematic function, in favor of Descartes, can be found in Jean-Luc Nancy, Corpus (New York: Fordham University Press, 2008) 136–44.

4. Jean-Paul Sartre, Being and Nothingness, trans. Hazel E. Barnes (New York: Washington Square Press, 1984), 441.

5. Pierre Guenancia, Lire Descartes (Paris: Gallimard, 2000), 244.

6. Descartes, The Passions of the Soul, 339.

7. René Descartes, "Letter to Princess Elisabeth (15 September 1645)," in Correspondences, 267.

8. Descartes, The Passions of the Soul, 379.

9. Guenancia, Lire Descartes, 250.

10. Guenancia, Lire Descartes, 251.

11. Guenancia, Lire Descartes, 254.

12. Descartes, The Passions of the Soul, 404, 348.

13. Descartes, The Passions of the Soul, 345.

14. René Descartes, "Conversation with Burman," trans. Jonathan Bennett, http://www.earlymoderntexts.com/assets/pdfs/descartes1648.pdf , 10, 11.

15. Descartes, The Passions of the Soul, 347.

16. Descartes, The Passions of the Soul, 381, 360.

17. Guenancia, Lire Descartes, 179.

18. Descartes, The Passions of the Soul, 347.

19. Descartes, The Passions of the Soul, 379, 380, 381.

20. Descartes, The Passions of the Soul, 379, 380.

21. René Descartes, Principles of Philosophy, in The Philosophical Writings, 1: 233.

22. Martial Guéroult, Descartes' Philosophy Interpreted According to the Order of Reasons, vol. 1: The Soul and God (Minneapolis: University of Minnesota Press, 1984) 105. See also Jean-Luc Marion, "Descartes Hors Sujet," Les études philosophiques 1, no. 88 (2009): 51–62.

23. Descartes, The Passions of the Soul, 380. See also Ernst Cassirer, Descartes: Lehre—Persönlichkeit—Wirkung (Hamburg: Meiner, 1995), 109.

24. Descartes, The Passions of the Soul, 380.

25. G. W. F. Hegel, Outlines of the Philosophy of Right, trans. T. M. Knox and Stephen Houlgate (Oxford: Oxford University Press, 2008), 38.

26. Descartes, The Passions of the Soul, 351.

27. Roberto Esposito, Communitas: The Origin and Destiny of Community (Stanford: Stanford University Press, 2010), 22.

28. Descartes, The Passions of the Soul, 351.

29. I owe this formulation to Jelica Šumič. Cf. Jelica Šumič, "The 21st Century Has Not Yet Begun," unpublished manuscript, 2010.

30. Jelica Šumič, "Contemporary Thought and the Crisis of Negation," Crisis and Critique 1, no. 3 (2014): 80.

31. Deborah J. Brown, Descartes and the Passionate Mind (Cambridge, UK: Cambridge University Press, 2006), 171.

32. G. W. F. Hegel, Vorlesungen über Rechtsphilosophie, 1818–1831, vol. 4 (Stuttgart: Fromman-Holzboog, 1974), 142.

33. Descartes, "Conversation with Burman," 11.

34. Descartes, The Passions of the Soul, 380.

35. Descartes, The Passions of the Soul, 380.

36. Descartes, "Conversation with Burman," 12.

37. Descartes, The Passions of the Soul, 380.

38. Descartes, The Passions of the Soul, 380–81.

39. Descartes, "Letter to Mersenne (9 January 1639)," in Correspondences, 131.

40. Descartes, The Passions of the Soul, 381.

41. Descartes, "Letter to [Vatier] (22 February 1638)," in Correspondences, 88.

42. René Descartes, "Letter to Elisabeth (6 October 1645)," in Oeuvres de Descartes, vol. 4, ed. C. Adam and P. Tannery (Paris: Vrin, 1976), 313–14.

43. René Descartes, Meditations on First Philosophy, in The Philosophical Writings of René Descartes, vol. 2, (Cambridge, UK: Cambridge University Press, 1984), 40.

44. Antonio Negri, The Political Descartes: Reason, Ideology and the Bourgeois Project (New York: Verso, 2007), 206.

45. Also see Jean-Luc Marion, Cartesian Questions (Chicago: University of Chicago Press, 1999), 139–60. A detailed discussion can also be

found in Jean-Luc Marion, Sur la théologie blanche de Descartes (Paris: puf, 1981).

46. For a more detailed rendering, see Guéroult, Descartes' Philosophy Interpreted According to the Order of Reasons.

47. René Descartes, Discourse on Method, in Philosophical Writings, 1:128–29.

48. Descartes, "Letter to Mersenne (27 May 1630)," in Correspondences, 25.

49. Alain Badiou, "Séminaire: Image du temps présent (1)," Entretemps, November 21, 2001, http://www.entretemps.asso.fr/Badiou /01-02.3.htm.

50. Alain Badiou, Being and Event (London: Continuum, 2008), 423.

51. Henri Gouhier, La pensée métaphysique de Descartes (Paris: Vrin, 1987), 291.

52. Descartes, Meditations on First Philosophy, in The Philosophical Writings, 2:32.

53. Jean-Paul Sartre, "Cartesian Freedom," in Literary and Philosophical Essays (Vancouver: Collier, 1967), 180–97.

54. See Harry Frankfurt, "Descartes on the Creation of Eternal Truths," Philosophical Review 96, no. 1 (1977): 36–57.

55. Descartes, "Letter to Mersenne (15 April 1630)," in Correspondences, 23.

56. Miran Božovič, Der große Andere: Gotteskonzepte in der Philosophie der Neuzeit (Vienna: Turia & Kant, 1993), 26–28.

57. Descartes, "Conversation with Burman," 12.

58. Gouhier, La pensée métaphysique de Descartes, 107.

59. Etienne Gilson, Etudes sur le role de la pensée médiévale dans la formation du système cartésien (Paris: Vrin, 1951), 224.

60. Descartes, Meditations on First Philosophy, 40–41.

61. Božovič, Der große Andere, 33.

62. Sartre, "Cartesian Freedom."

63. Descartes, The Passions of the Soul, 351.

64. Pierre Guenancia, "Descartes: Jusqu'à son installation en Hollande," Les Auteurs en Touraine, http://mapage.noos.fr/crosin000v /Descartes/Extraits_fr_Descartes.html.

3. FROM KANT TO SCHMID (AND BACK)

Denis Diderot, *Jacques the Fatalist and His Master* (London: Penguin, 1986), 161; Theodor W. Adorno, *Problems of Moral Philosophy* (Stanford: Stanford University Press, 2001), 2–3; Immanuel Kant, "Conjectural Beginning of Human History," in *Anthropology, History, Education* (Cambridge, UK: Cambridge University Press, 2007), 173.

1. Immanuel Kant, *Groundwork of the Metaphysics of Morals*, trans. Mary Gregor (Cambridge, UK: Cambridge University Press, 1998), 22.

2. Kant, *Groundwork of the Metaphysics of Morals*, 19, 20.

3. Kant, *Groundwork of the Metaphysics of Morals*, 20, 21.

4. Kant, *Groundwork of the Metaphysics of Morals*, 22, 35.

5. Kant, *Groundwork of the Metaphysics of Morals*, 23, 24.

6. Kant, *Groundwork of the Metaphysics of Morals*, 25, 26, 27, 30, 31.

7. Immanuel Kant, *Critique of Pure Reason* (Cambridge, UK: Cambridge University Press, 1998), 143. See also Slavoj Žižek, *Tarrying with the Negative: Kant, Hegel and the Critique of Ideology* (Durham NC: Duke University Press, 1998), 13–14.

8. Kant, *Groundwork of the Metaphysics of Morals*, 30, 31, 44, 45, 47.

9. Rado Riha, "Handeln, 'ob ich gleich nichts anderes wollte': Kants praktische Philosophie als Theorie des subjektivierenden Handelns," *Filozofski vestnik* 26, no. 2 (2005): 44.

10. Kant, *Groundwork of the Metaphysics of Morals*, 35.

11. Riha, "Handeln," 44.

12. Kant, *Groundwork of the Metaphysics of Morals*, 52, 53.

13. Kant, *Groundwork of the Metaphysics of Morals*, 56

14. Alenka Zupančič, *Ethics of the Real: Kant, Lacan* (London: Verso, 2000), 37.

15. Nicole Loraux, *The Divided City: On Memory and Forgetting in Ancient Athens*, trans. Corinne Pache and Jeff Fort (New York: Zone, 2001).

16. Kant, *Groundwork of the Metaphysics of Morals*, 65, 66.

17. Carl Christian Erhard Schmid, *Versuch einer Moralphilosophie*, 2nd ed. (Jena: Crökersche Handlung, 1790), 1.

18. Carl Christian Erhard Schmid, *Versuch einer Moralphilosophie*, 3rd ed. (Jena: Crökersche Handlung, 1792), 12; Schmid, *Versuch einer Moralphilosophie* (1790), 3.

19. Schmid, *Versuch einer Moralphilosophie* (1790), 5–6, 7, 11.

20. Schmid, *Versuch einer Moralphilosophie* (1790), 10, 32, 36, 17, 26.

21. Schmid, *Versuch einer Moralphilosophie* (1792), 78.

22. Schmid, *Versuch einer Moralphilosophie* (1790), 27, 47.

23. Schmid, *Versuch einer Moralphilosophie* (1792), 126–41, 141–77.

24. Schmid, *Versuch einer Moralphilosophie* (1790), 84, 99, 95, 69.

25. Schmid, *Versuch einer Moralphilosophie* (1790), 99–100.

26. Schmid, *Versuch einer Moralphilosophie* (1792), 185.

27. Schmid, *Versuch einer Moralphilosophie* (1790), 100.

28. Schmid, *Versuch einer Moralphilosophie* (1790), 102, 104, 110, 111, 116.

29. Schmid, *Versuch einer Moralphilosophie* (1790), 123, 127, 128, 134, 136, 141, 143, 148.

30. Schmid, *Versuch einer Moralphilosophie* (1790), 157.

31. Alain Badiou, *Theory of the Subject*, trans. Bruno Bosteels (London: Continuum, 2009), 3–12.

32. Schmid, *Versuch einer Moralphilosophie* (1790), 159.

33. Schmid, *Versuch einer Moralphilosophie* (1790), 165, 166, 168, 176.

34. Carl Christian Erhard Schmid, "Die Wege der Vorsehung," in *Predigten* (Jena: Stahl, 1797), 239–52.

35. Schmid, *Versuch einer Moralphilosophie* (1790), 177, 178, 181; Schmid, *Versuch einer Moralphilosophie* (1792), 300–302.

36. Immanuel Kant, "What Does It Mean to Orient Oneself in Thinking?," in *Religion and Rational Theology* (Cambridge, UK: Cambridge University Press, 1996), 10.

37. Schmid, *Versuch einer Moralphilosophie* (1790), 180, 183.

38. Schmid, *Versuch einer Moralphilosophie* (1790), 187, 188, 190.

39. Schmid, *Versuch einer Moralphilosophie* (1792), 344.

40. Schmid, *Versuch einer Moralphilosophie* (1790), 196, 198.

41. Schmid, *Versuch einer Moralphilosophie* (1792), 341–42, 335–37.

42. Carl Christian Erhard Schmid, "Vorrede," in Leonhard Creuzer, *Skeptische Betrachtungen über die Freiheit des Willens mit Hinsicht auf die neueste Theorie über dieselbe* (Gießen: Heyer, 1793), ix.

43. Schmid, *Versuch einer Moralphilosophie* (1790), 211; (1792), 388.

44. Schmid, "Vorrede," x.

45. Schmid, *Versuch einer Moralphilosophie* (1792), 389.

46. Schmid, *Versuch einer Moralphilosophie* (1790), 215, 209.

47. Schmid, *Versuch einer Moralphilosophie* (1792), 388.

48. Josef Pieper, *The End of Time: A Meditation on the Philosophy of History* (San Francisco: Ignatius, 1999), 84. See also Peter Fenves, *Late Kant: Towards Another Law of the Earth* (London: Routledge, 2003), 143–50.

49. Immanuel Kant, "The End of All Things," in *Religion and Rational Theology*, 221.

50. See Giorgio Agamben, *The Time That Remains: A Commentary on the Letter to the Romans*, trans. Patricia Dailey (Stanford: Stanford University Press, 2005), 62–69.

51. Kant, "The End of All Things," 221, 224.

52. See also Ray Brassier, *Nihil Unbound: Enlightenment and Extinction* (New York: Palgrave, 2007).

53. Kant, "The End of All Things," 222.

4. ENDING WITH THE WORST

Denis Diderot, *Jacques the Fatalist and His Master* (London: Penguin, 1986), 234; Rainer Maria Rilke, *Duino Elegies* (New York: Vintage International 2009), 53; G. W. F. Hegel, *Phenomenology of Spirit*, trans. A. V. Miller (Oxford: Oxford University Press, 1977), 19.

1. Fredric Jameson, *The Hegel Variations: On the Phenomenology of Spirit* (New York: Verso, 2010), 54.

2. Cf. Ernst Cassirer, *The Problem of Knowledge: Philosophy, Science and History since Hegel*, trans. William H. Woglom (New Haven CT: Yale University Press 1969), 159; Karl Marx, *Critique of Hegel's Doctrine of the State* (1843), in *Early Writings*, trans. Rodney Livingstone and Gregor Benton (London: Penguin, 1992), 108.

3. Jürgen Habermas, "Hegel's Critique of the French Revolution," in *Theory and Practice*, trans. John Viertel (Boston: Beacon, 1973), 139.

4. One can find such a reading in Giorgio Agamben, *Language and Death: The Place of Negativity*, trans. Michael Hardt (Minneapolis: University of Minnesota Press, 2006).

5. See Howard Sherman, "Marx and Determinism," *Journal of Economic Issues* 15, no. 1 (1981): 63–64. For a different perspective, see Roland Boer, "Marxism and Eschatology Reconsidered," *Mediations: Journal of the Marxist Literary Group* 25, no. 1 (2010), http://www.mediations journal.org/toc/25_1.

6. For a different reading, see Catherine Malabou, *The Future of Hegel: Plasticity, Temporality and Dialectic*, trans. Lisabeth During (New York: Routledge, 2004).

7. Jacques Lacan, *The Seminar of Jacques Lacan*, book 20: *Encore 1972–1973*, trans. Bruce Fink (New York: Norton, 1999), 55.

8. Jonathan Lear, *Happiness, Death, and the Remainder of Life* (Cambridge MA: Harvard University Press, 2000), 129. On the "too much" of too much, see Eric L. Santner, *On the Psychotheology of Everyday Life: Reflections on Freud and Rosenzweig* (Chicago: University of Chicago Press, 2001).

9. See Eckart Förster, *The Twenty-Five Years of Philosophy: A Systematic Reconstruction*, trans. Brady Bowman (Cambridge MA: Harvard University Press, 2012).

10. G. W. F. Hegel, *Lectures on the History of Philosophy: Greek Philosophy to Plato*, trans. E. S. Haldane (Lincoln: University of Nebraska Press, 1995), 52.

11. See G. W. F. Hegel, *Werke*, vol. 4: *Philosophische Enzyklopädie für die Oberklasse (1808ff.)* (Frankfurt am Main: Suhrkamp, 1986), 13.

12. G. F. W. Hegel, *The Philosophy of History*, trans. J. Sibree (Ontario: Kitchener, 2001), 88.

13. Hegel, *The Philosophy of History*, 85, 90, 95.

14. Hegel, *The Philosophy of History*, 96.

15. G. W. F. Hegel, *Outlines* of the Philosophy of Right, trans. T. M. Knox and Stephen Houlgate (Oxford: Oxford University Press, 2008), 16.

16. Hegel, *The Philosophy of History*, 35.

17. Hegel, *Outlines*, 16. See also Hegel, *Lectures on the History of Philosophy*, 52. For a discussion of "grey on grey," see Rebecca Comay, *Mourning Sickness: Hegel and the French Revolution* (Stanford: Stanford University Press, 2011), 144.

18. Robert Pippin, "Back to Hegel?," *Mediations* 26, nos. 1–2 (2013), http://www.mediationsjournal.org/articles/back-to-hegel.

19. I owe this wonderful formulation to Mladen Dolar.

20. Jacob Taubes, *Occidental Eschatology*, trans. David Ratmoko (Stanford: Stanford University Press, 2009), 90–97, 149–63.

21. Karl Löwith, *From Hegel to Nietzsche: The Revolution in Nineteenth-Century Thought*, trans. David E. Green (New York: Columbia

University Press, 1964), 35. Also see Karl Löwith, *Weltgeschichte als Heilsgeschichte: Zur Kritik der Geschichtsphilosophie* (Stuttgart: Metzler, 1983), 224–25.

22. Malcolm Bull, *Seeing Things Hidden: Apocalypse, Vision and Totality* (New York: Verso, 1999), 100, 113.

23. Hegel, *Outlines*, 16.

24. G. W. F. Hegel, "Letter to Tholuck (July 3rd, 1826)," in *Hegel: The Letters*, trans. Clark Butler and Christine Seiler (Bloomington: Indiana University Press, 1984), 520.

25. Hegel, *Outlines*, 16.

26. Terry Pinkard, *Hegel's Naturalism: Mind, Nature, and the Final Ends of Life* (Oxford: Oxford University Press, 2013).

27. G. W. F. Hegel, *Encyclopedia of the Philosophical Sciences in Basic Outline*, part 1: *Science of Logic*, trans. Klaus Brinkmann and Daniel O. Dahlstrom (Cambridge, UK: Cambridge University Press, 2010), 219–20.

28. G. W. F. Hegel, *Science of Logic* (New York: Humanity, 1969), 444. For this also see Slavoj Žižek, *Absolute Recoil: Towards a New Foundation of Dialectical Materialism* (London: Verso, 2014).

29. G. W. F. Hegel, "Review, *Friedrich Heinrich Jacobi's Works, Volume III*," in *Heidelberg Writings*, trans. Brady Bowman and Allen Speight (Cambridge, UK: Cambridge University Press, 2015), 11, translation altered.

30. Hegel, *Outlines*, 307.

31. G. W. F. Hegel, *The Philosophy of Mind: The Encyclopedia of Philosophical Sciences*, book 3 (Oxford: Clarendon, 1971), 59.

32. G. W. F. Hegel, *The Difference between Fichte's and Schelling's System of Philosophy*, trans. Walter Cerf and H. S. Harris (Albany: State University of New York Press, 1977), 117, translation altered.

33. Hegel, *The Philosophy of History*, 24–25.

34. Hegel, *Science of Logic*, 50.

35. Hegel, *The Philosophy of History*, 28, 477, 34.

36. Hegel, *Outlines*, 46.

37. Hegel, *The Philosophy of History*, 24.

38. Hegel, *Science of Logic*, 487.

39. Hegel, *The Philosophy of History*, 51.

40. Hegel, *The Philosophy of History*, 28.

41. Hegel, *Science of Logic*, 69.

42. Hegel, *The Philosophy of History*, 23.

43. Slavoj Žižek, *Less Than Nothing: Hegel and the Shadow of Dialectical Materialism* (New York: Verso, 2012), 528.

44. E. Gordon Rupp and Philip S. Watson, eds., *Luther and Erasmus: Free Will and Salvation* (Louisville KY: Westminster, 1996), 213.

45. Hegel, *Lectures on the History of Philosophy*, 35.

46. Hegel, *The Philosophy of History*, 19, 23.

47. Žižek, *Less than Nothing*, 377.

48. See Alenka Zupančič, *The Odd One In: On Comedy* (Cambridge MA: MIT Press, 2008), 15.

49. Rebecca Comay, "Resistance and Repetition: Freud and Hegel," *Research in Phenomenology* 45 (2015): 262, 266.

50. See Zupančič, *The Odd One In*, 39.

51. Hegel, *Phenomenology of Spirit*, 492, 493.

52. See Dieter Henrich, "Hegels Theorie über den Zufall," in *Hegel im Kontext* (Frankfurt am Main: Suhrkamp, 1975), 157–86.

53. Hegel, *Science of Logic*, 69.

54. Hegel, *Phenomenology of Spirit*, 492, 491.

55. Slavoj Žižek, *The Sublime Object* (New York: Verso, 2002), 221.

5. AFTER THE END

Denis Diderot, *Jacques the Fatalist and His Master* (London: Penguin, 1986), 236; Sigmund Freud, "Delusions and Dreams in Jensen's Gradiva," in *The Standard Edition of the Complete Psychological Works of Sigmund Freud*, ed. James Strachey, vol. 9: *Jensen's "Gradiva" and Other Works* (London: Hogarth, 1959), 9; Jacob Taubes, "Religion und die Zukunft der Psychoanalyse," in *Psychoanalyse und Religion*, ed. Eckart Nase and Joachim Scharfenberg (Darmstadt: Wiss. Buchgesellschaft, 1977), 175.

1. Sigmund Freud, *Introductory Lectures on Psycho-Analysis* (New York: Norton, 1966), 31, 32, 33.

2. Sigmund Freud, "Recommendations to Physicians Practicing Psychoanalysis," in *The Standard Edition of the Complete Psychological Works of Sigmund Freud*, ed. James Strachey, vol. 12: *The Case of Schreber, Papers on Technique, and Other Works* (London: Hogarth, 1958), 115.

3. Sigmund Freud, "Recommendations to Physicians Practising Psycho-Analysis," in *The Standard Edition of the Complete Psychological Works of Sigmund Freud*, 12: 111-13.

4. For the meaning of an "operational" concept, see Alain Badiou, *Being and Event* (London: Continuum, 2008), 65.

5. Freud, *Introductory Lectures on Psycho-Analysis*, 33.

6. Freud, *Introductory Lectures on Psycho-Analysis*, 37–38, 49 115, 109.

7. Alain Badiou, "L'immanence des vérités: Séminaire d'Alain Badiou (2012–2013)," http://www.entretemps.asso.fr/Badiou/12-13.htm.

8. Jacques Lacan, "The Function and Field of Speech and Language in Psychoanalysis," in *Écrits*, trans. Bruce Fink (New York: Norton, 2006), 253.

9. Sigmund Freud, "The Uncanny," in *The Standard Edition of the Complete Psychological Works of Sigmund Freud*, ed. James Strachey, vol. 17: *An Infantile Neurosis and Other Works* (London: Hogarth, 1955), 245.

10. Sigmund Freud, *The Interpretation of Dreams*, in *The Standard Edition of the Complete Psychological Works of Sigmund Freud*, ed. James Strachey, vol. 5: *The Interpretation of Dreams (Second Part)* (London: Hogarth, 1958), 612.

11. Freud, *Introductory Lectures on Psycho-Analysis*, 179.

12. Freud, *Introductory Lectures on Psycho-Analysis*, 59.

13. Stanley Cavell, *Pursuits of Happiness: The Hollywood Comedies of Remarriage* (Cambridge MA: Harvard University Press, 1984), 96.

14. Freud, *Introductory Lectures on Psycho-Analysis*, 32.

15. Octave Mannoni, *Freud* (New York: Pantheon, 1971), 82.

16. Freud, *Introductory Lectures on Psycho-Analysis*, 130.

17. Sigmund Freud, *New Introductory Lectures on Psycho-Analysis* (New York: Norton, 1965), 152.

18. Freud, *The Interpretation of Dreams*, in *The Standard Edition of the Complete Psychological Works of Sigmund Freud*, 5: 614.

19. Sigmund Freud, "The Future of an Illusion," in *The Standard Edition of the Complete Psychological Works of Sigmund Freud*, ed. James Strachey, vol. 21: *The "Future of an Illusion," "Civilization and Its Discontents" and Other Works* (London: Hogarth Press, 1961), 32.

20. Freud, "The Future of an Illusion," 56.

21. Freud, "The Future of an Illusion," 30.

22. Freud, *New Introductory Lectures on Psycho-Analysis*, 207.

23. Sigmund Freud, "The Theme of the Three Caskets," in *The Standard Edition of the Complete Psychological Works of Sigmund Freud*, 12: 299.

24. Freud, "The Future of an Illusion," 47.

25. Freud, *Introductory Lectures on Psycho-Analysis*, 238.

26. See Jacques Lacan, "Presentation on Psychical Causality," in *Écrits*, 123–60. See also Freud, *Introductory Lectures on Psycho-Analysis*, 445–68.

27. Freud, *Introductory Lectures on Psycho-Analysis*, 445–68.

28. Mladen Dolar, "What's the Matter? On Matter and Related Matters," unpublished manuscript.

29. Freud, *Introductory Lectures on Psycho-Analysis*, 68.

30. Sigmund Freud, *The Psychopathology of Everyday Life* (1901), in *The Standard Edition of the Complete Psychological Works of Sigmund Freud*, ed. James Strachey, vol. 6: *The Psychopathology of Everyday Life* (London: Hogarth, 1960), 4, 6, 191, 192, 199.

31. Freud, *Psychopathology*, 214; Jacques Lacan, *The Seminar of Jacques Lacan*, book 1: *Freud's Papers on Technique* (New York: Norton, 1991), 16.

32. Freud, *Psychopathology*, 214, 209, 240, 215.

33. Freud, *Psychopathology*, 240, 253, 254.

34. Freud, *Psychopathology*, 254.

35. Freud, *Psychopathology*, 147.

36. Freud, *Psychopathology*, 254.

37. R. Andrew Paskauskas, ed., *The Complete Correspondence of Sigmund Freud and Ernest Jones, 1908–1939* (Cambridge MA: Belknap, 1995), 100.

38. Sigmund Freud, "Two Encyclopedia Articles," in *The Standard Edition of the Complete Psychological Works of Sigmund Freud*, ed. James Strachey, vol. 18: *Beyond the Pleasure Principle, Group Psychology, and Other Works* (London: Hogarth Press, 1955), 238.

39. Jacques Lacan, "Beyond the Reality Principle," in *Écrits*, 81–82.

40. Sigmund Freud, "On Beginning the Treatment (Further Recommendations on the Technique of Psycho-Analysis I)," in *The Standard Edition of the Complete Psychological Works of Sigmund Freud*, 12: 134.

41. Freud, "On Beginning the Treatment," 134–35.

42. Lacan, *Seminar*, 265.

43. Freud, "On Beginning the Treatment," 135.

44. Freud, "Two Encyclopedia Articles," 238.

45. Comay, "Resistance and Repetition: Freud and Hegel," 247.

46. Comay, "Resistance and Repetition," 247.

47. Sigmund Freud, "An Autobiographical Study," in *The Standard Edition of the Complete Psychological Works of Sigmund Freud*, ed. James Strachey, vol. 20: *An Autobiographical Study; Inhibitions, Symptoms and Anxiety; The Question of Lay Analysis; and Other Works* (London: Hogarth, 1966), 40–41.

48. Mladen Dolar, *A Voice and Nothing More* (Cambridge MA: MIT Press 2006), 158.

49. Freud, *Introductory Lectures on Psycho-Analysis*, 184.

50. Freud, *Introductory Lectures on Psycho-Analysis*, 540, translation altered.

51. Sigmund Freud, "On the Universal Tendency to Debasement in the Sphere of Love Life," in *The Standard Edition of the Complete Psychological Works of Sigmund Freud*, ed. James Strachey, vol. 11: *Five Lectures on Psycho-Analysis, Leonardo da Vinci and Other Works* (London: Hogarth, 1957), 186.

52. Freud, "Delusions and Dreams in Jensen's Gradiva," 9.

53. Sigmund Freud, "Instincts and Their Vicissitudes," in *The Standard Edition of the Complete Psychological Works of Sigmund Freud*, ed. James Strachey, vol. 14: *On the History of the Post Psycho-Analytic Movement, Papers on Metapsychology and Other Works* (London: Hogarth, 1966), 118–19. We here move from *Grundregel* to *Grundbegriff*.

54. Freud, "Instincts and Their Vicissitudes," 124. See also Jacques Lacan, *The Seminar of Jacques Lacan*, book 9: *The Four Fundamental Concepts of Psychoanalysis* (New York: Norton, 1978), 162–73.

55. Freud, "Instincts and Their Vicissitudes," 127.

56. Slavoj Žižek, *The Ticklish Subject: The Absent Centre of Political Ontology* (New York: Verso, 1999), 303.

57. Sigmund Freud, "Repression," in *The Standard Edition of the Complete Psychological Works of Sigmund Freud*, 14: 149.

58. Sigmund Freud, *The Interpretation of Dreams*, in *The Standard Edition of the Complete Psychological Works of Sigmund Freud*, ed. James Strachey, vol. 4: *The Interpretation of Dreams (First Part)* (London: Hogarth, 1953), 262.

59. Sigmund Freud, "The Question of Lay Analysis," in *The Standard Edition of the Complete Psychological Works of Sigmund Freud*, 20: 213.

60. Freud, *New Introductory Lectures on Psycho-Analysis*, 133.

61. Sigmund Freud, "The Dissolution of the Oedipus Complex," in *The Standard Edition of the Complete Psychological Works of Sigmund Freud*, ed. James Strachey, vol. 19: *The Ego and the Id and Other Works* (London: Hogarth, 1961), 173–79.

62. J. W. Goethe, *Werke*, vol. 10: *Autobiographische Schriften 2* (Hamburg: Beck, 2002), 546.

63. Freud, "On the Universal Tendency to Debasement," 189. The article is omitted in the English translation.

64. G. W. F. Hegel, *The Philosophy of History*, trans. J. Sibree (Ontario: Kitchener, 2001), 296.

65. Freud, "On the Universal Tendency to Debasement," 188–89.

66. Freud, "On the Universal Tendency to Debasement," 189.

67. Toril Moi, "Is Anatomy Destiny? Freud and Biological Determinism," in *Whose Freud? The Place of Psychoanalysis in Contemporary Culture*, ed. Peter Brooks and Alex Woloch (New Haven CT: Yale University Press, 2000), 79.

68. Slavoj Žižek, *Less than Nothing: Hegel and the Shadow of Dialectical Materialism* (New York: Verso, 2012), 216.

69. Freud, "The Dissolution of the Oedipus Complex," 177, 175.

70. Sigmund Freud, "The Question of Lay Analysis," in *The Standard Edition of the Complete Psychological Works of Sigmund Freud*, 20: 213.

71. Freud, "The Dissolution of the Oedipus Complex," 177, 178.

72. Sigmund Freud, "Some Psychical Consequences of the Anatomical Distinction between the Sexes," in *The Standard Edition of the Complete Psychological Works of Sigmund Freud*, 19: 126.

73. Sigmund Freud, "The Disposition to Obsessional Neurosis: A Contribution to the Problem of Choice of Neurosis," in *The Standard Edition of the Complete Psychological Works of Sigmund Freud*, 12: 317.

74. Alenka Zupančič, *Ethics of the Real: Kant and Lacan* (New York: Verso, 2000), 35.

75. Zupančič, *Ethics of the Real*, 39.

LAST WORDS

Samuel Beckett, *The Unnameable*, in *Three Novels* (New York: Grove, 2009), 403.

1. Bertolt Brecht, "On Hegelian Dialectic," Autodidact Project, http://www.autodidactproject.org/other/hegel-brecht.html.

2. Jacques Lacan, *The Seminar of Jacques Lacan*, book 17: *The Other Side of Psychoanalysis* (New York: Norton, 2007), 192.

3. Alenka Zupančič, *The Odd One In: On Comedy* (Cambridge MA: MIT Press, 2008), 13.

4. G. W. F. Hegel, "On the Scientific Ways of Treating Natural Law, on Its Place in Practical Philosophy, and Its Relation to the Positive Science of Right," in *Political Writings* (Cambridge, UK: Cambridge University Press, 1999), 152–53.

5. G. W. F. Hegel, *Hegel's Aesthetics: Lectures on Fine Art*, trans. T. M. Know (Oxford: Oxford University Press, 1975), 1199.

6. Zupančič, *The Odd One In*, 29.

7. Hegel, *Hegel's Aesthetics*, 1199.

8. Immanuel Kant, *Critique of Judgment* (Indianapolis: Hackett, 1987), 203.

9. Hegel, *Hegel's Aesthetics*, 1200, 1202.

10. Hegel, *Hegel's Aesthetics*, 1233, 1220.

11. Zupančič, *The Odd One In*, 66–67, 176–77.

12. Friedrich Nietzsche, *Nachlaß 1869–1874*, in *Kritische Studienausgabe*, vol. 7 (Munich: de Gruyter 1999), 431.

IN THE PROVOCATIONS SERIES

*Abolishing Freedom: A Plea for a
Contemporary Use of Fatalism*
Frank Ruda

To order or obtain more information on these or other University of
Nebraska Press titles, visit nebraskapress.unl.edu.